Jellyfish Adult Coloring Book

This Coloring book belongs to:

____

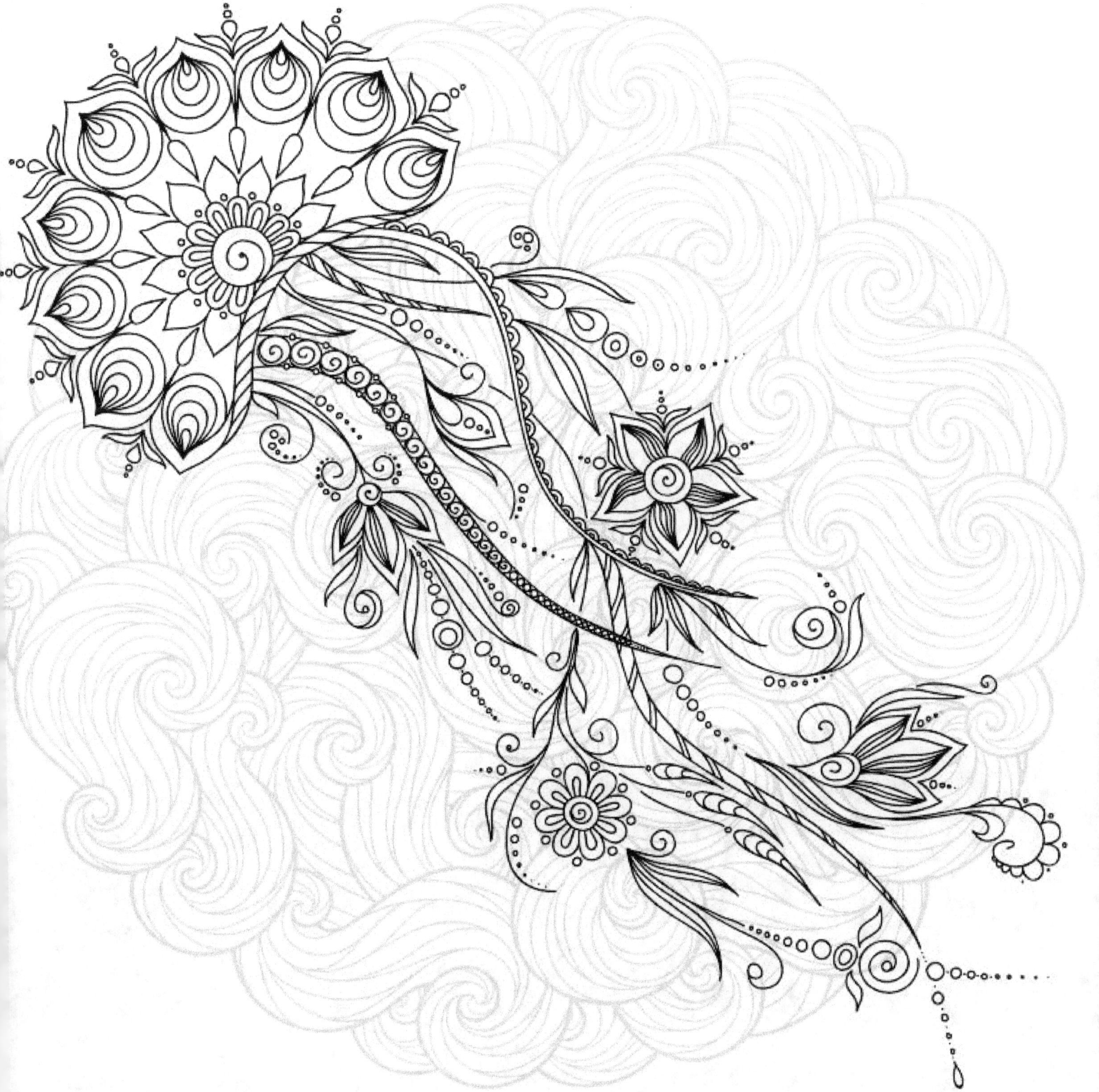

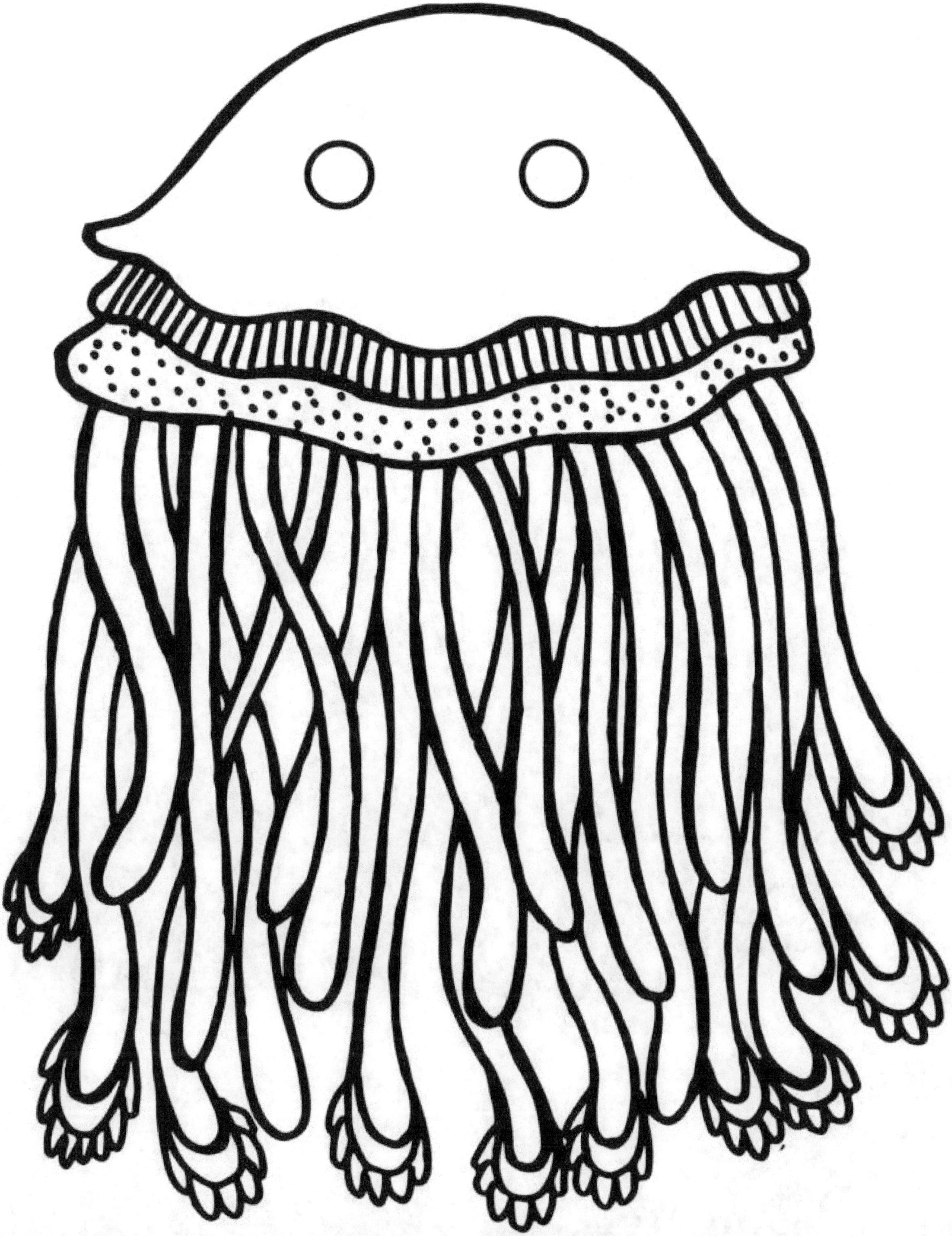

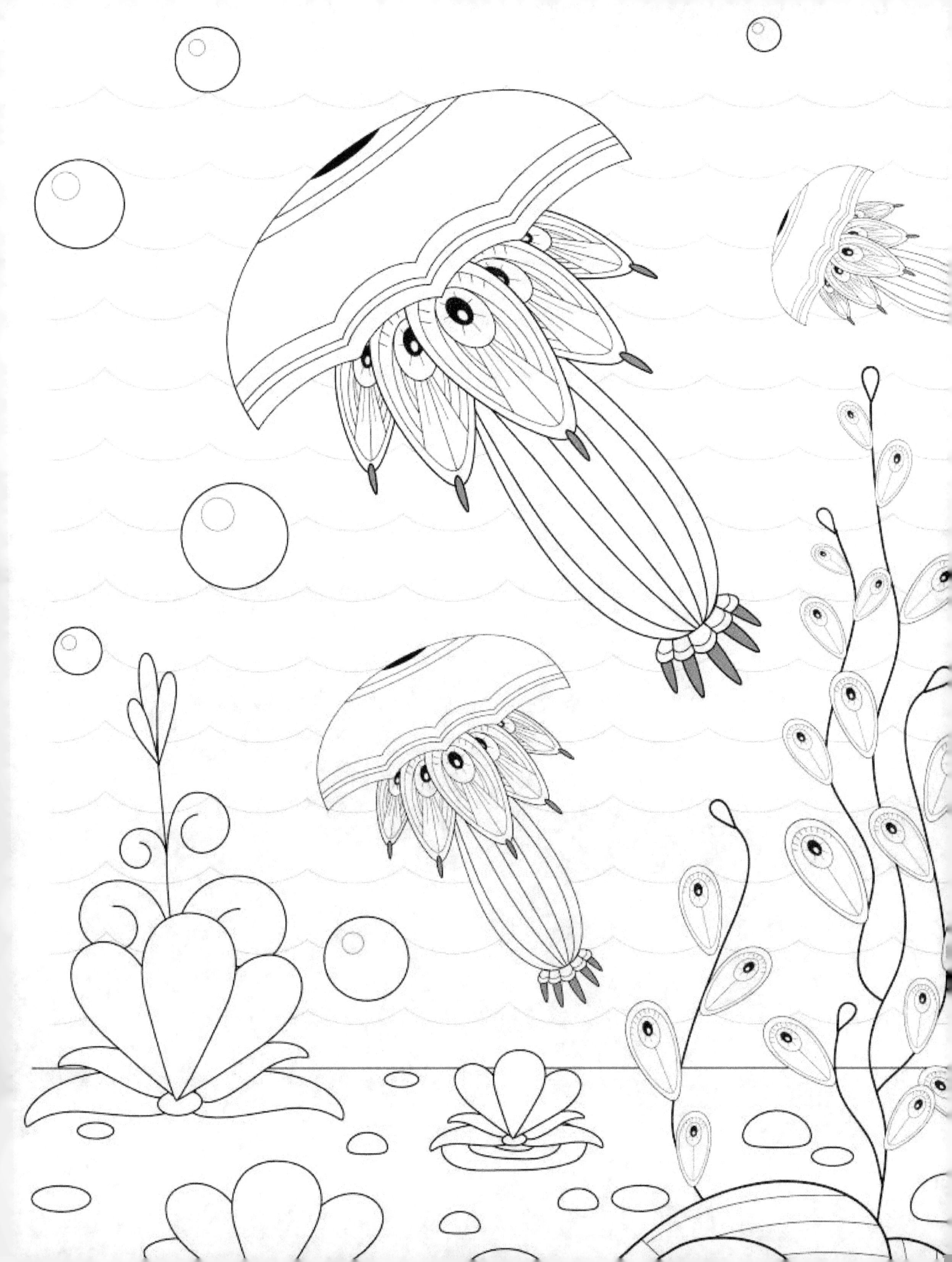

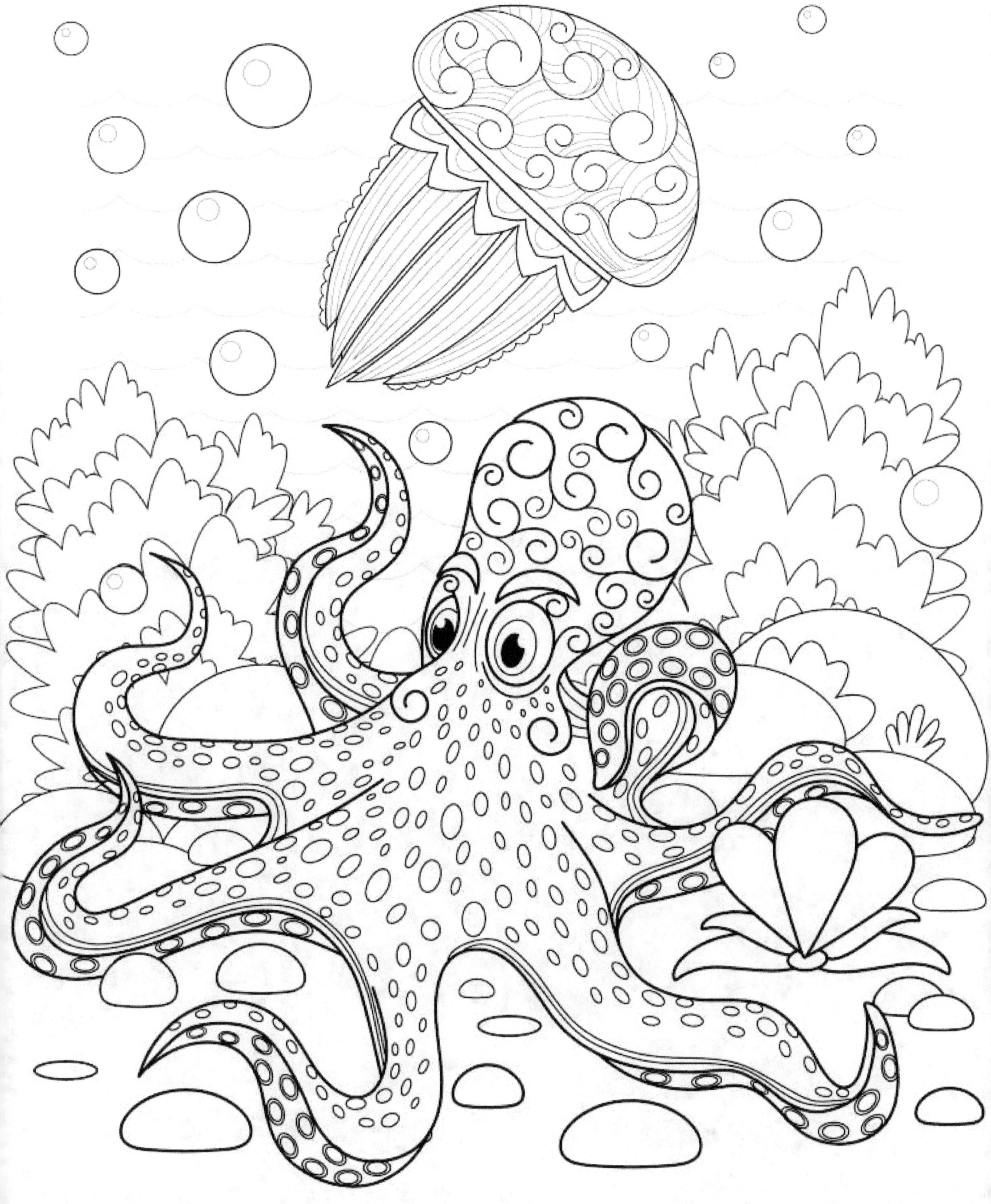

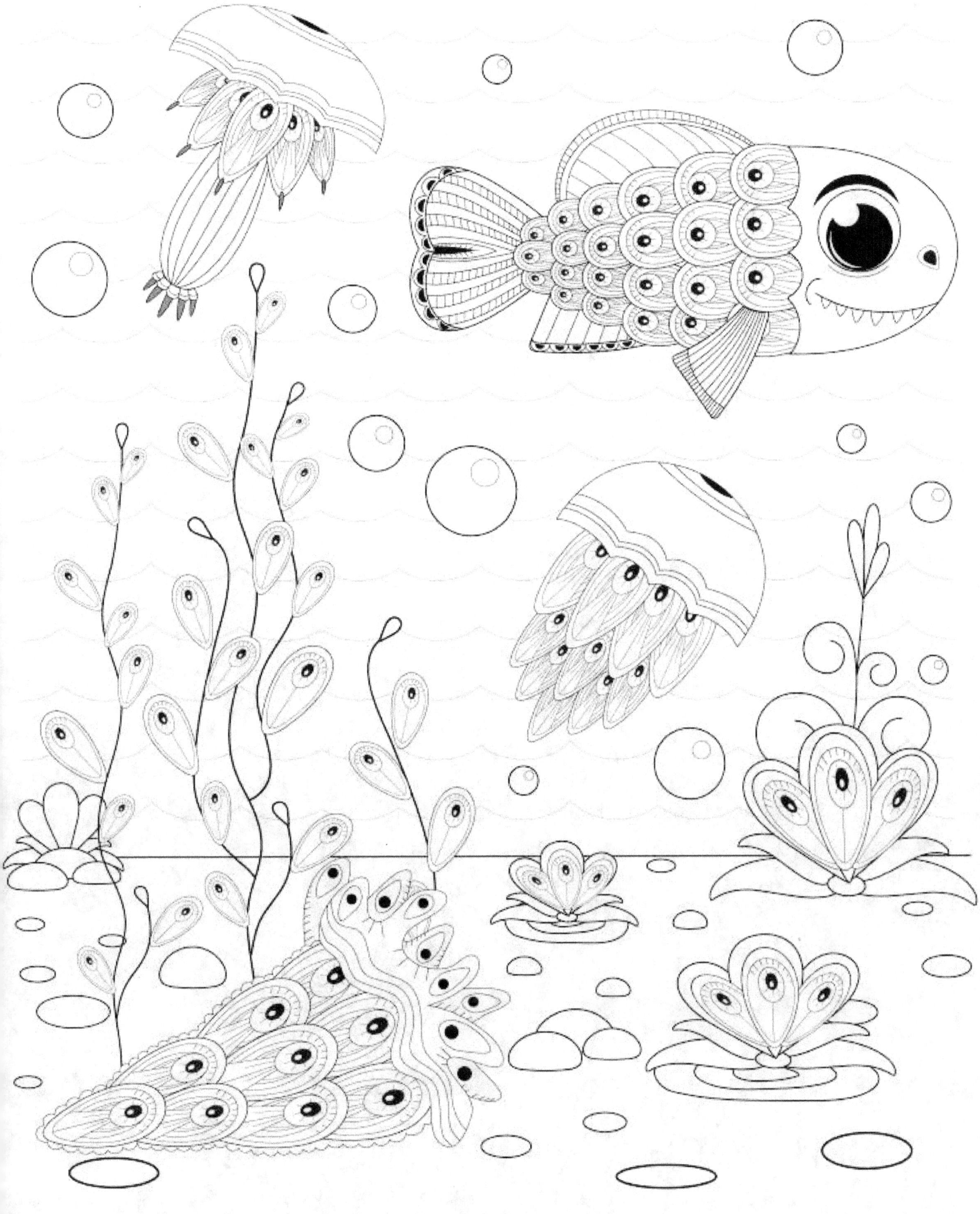

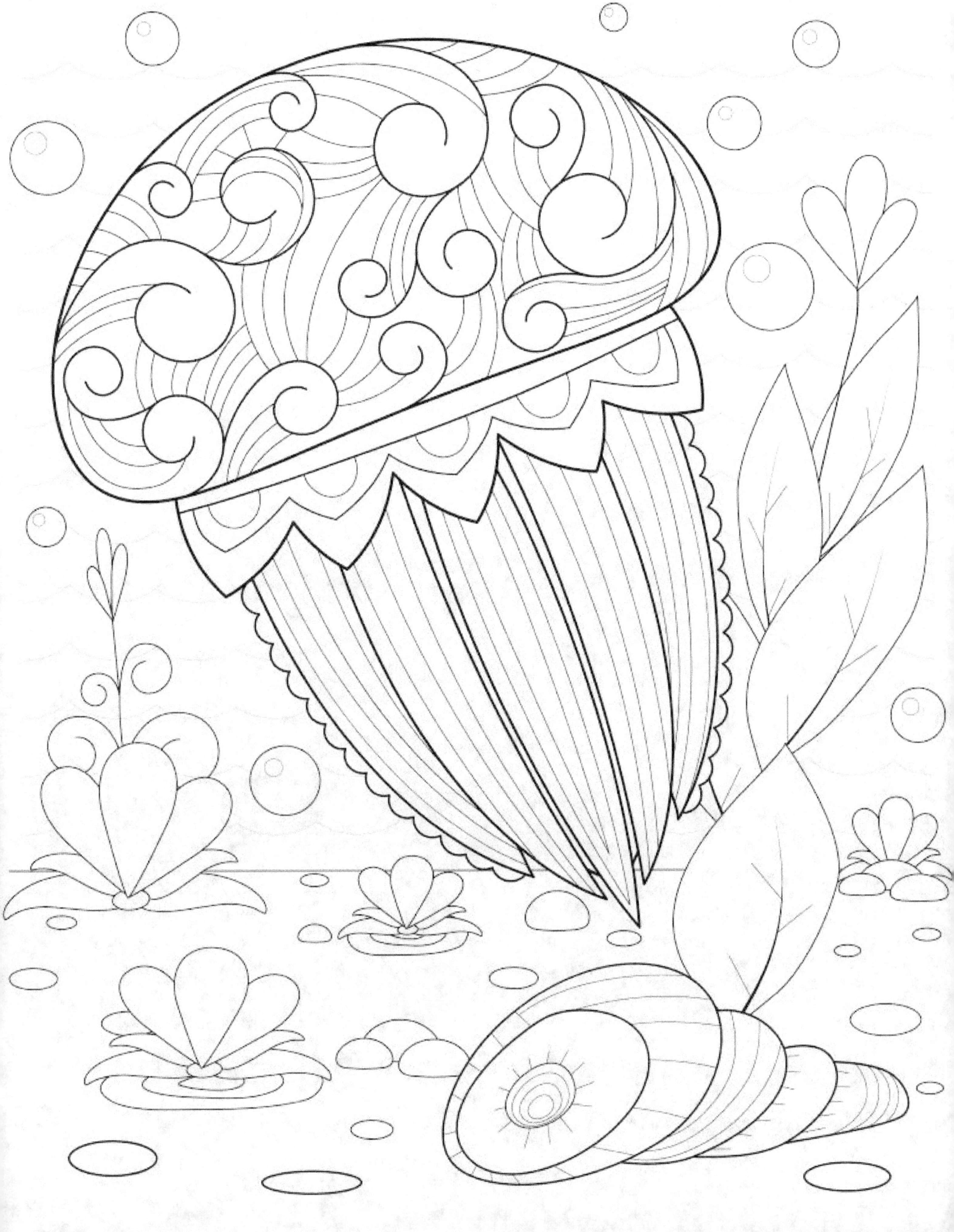

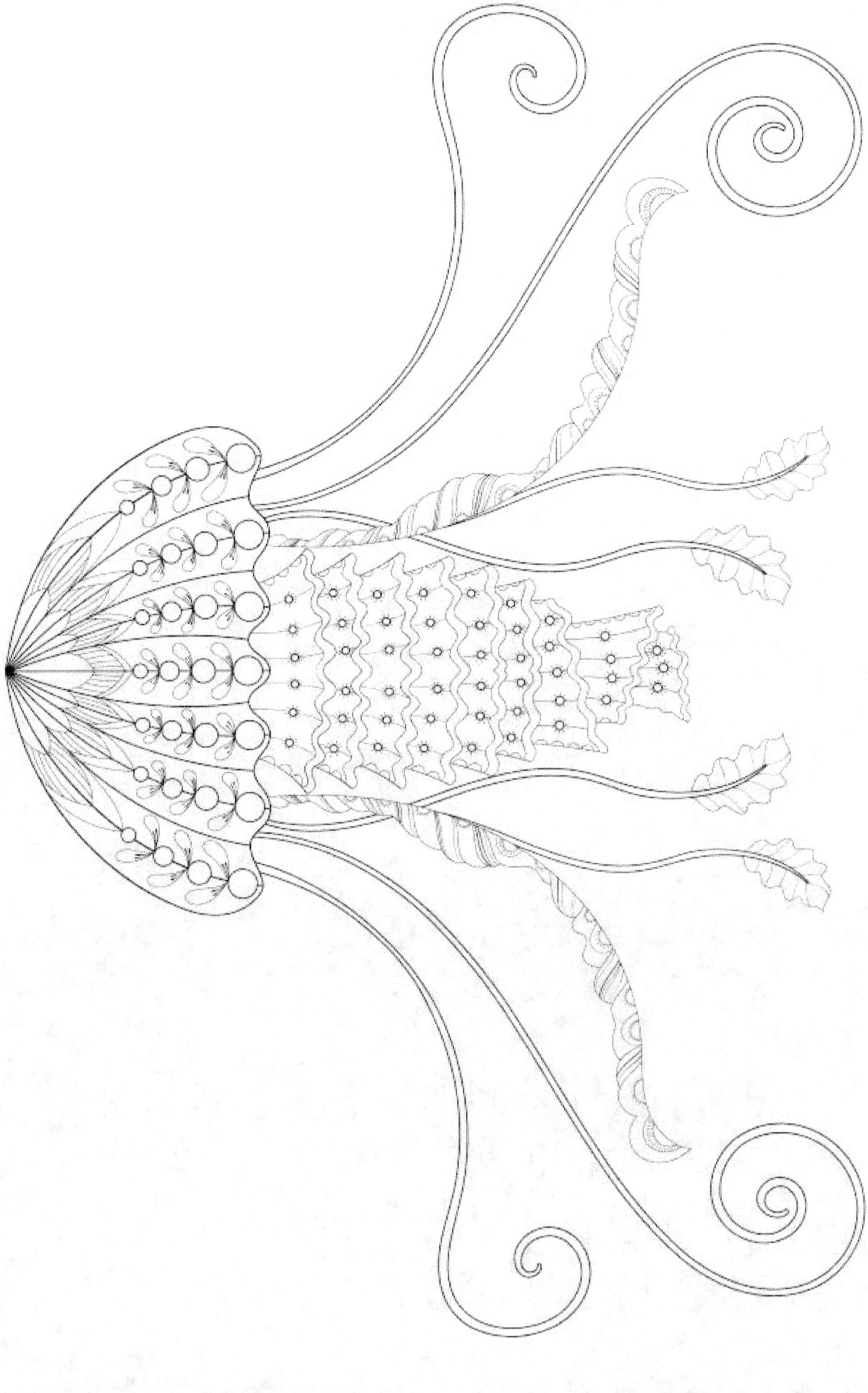

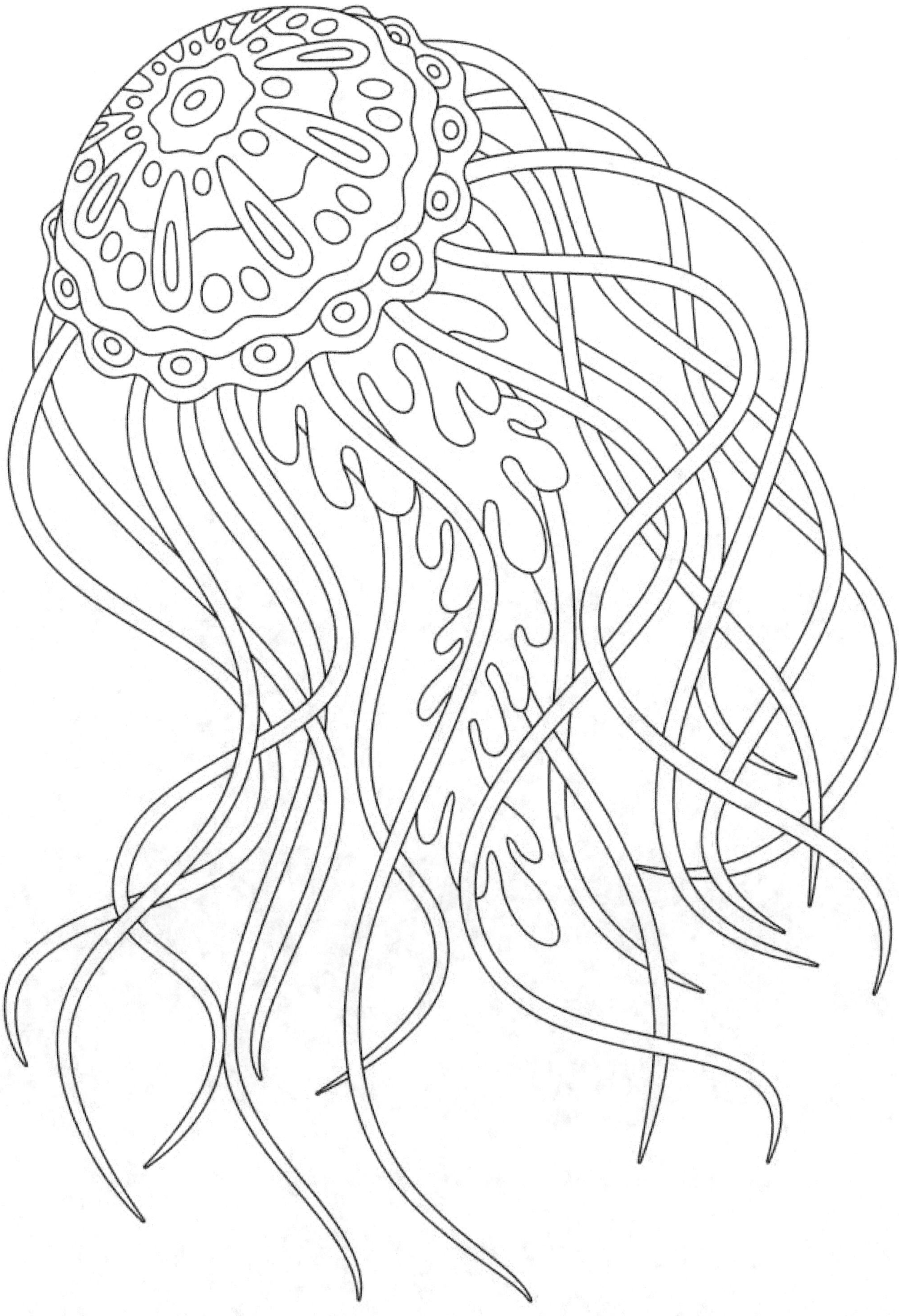

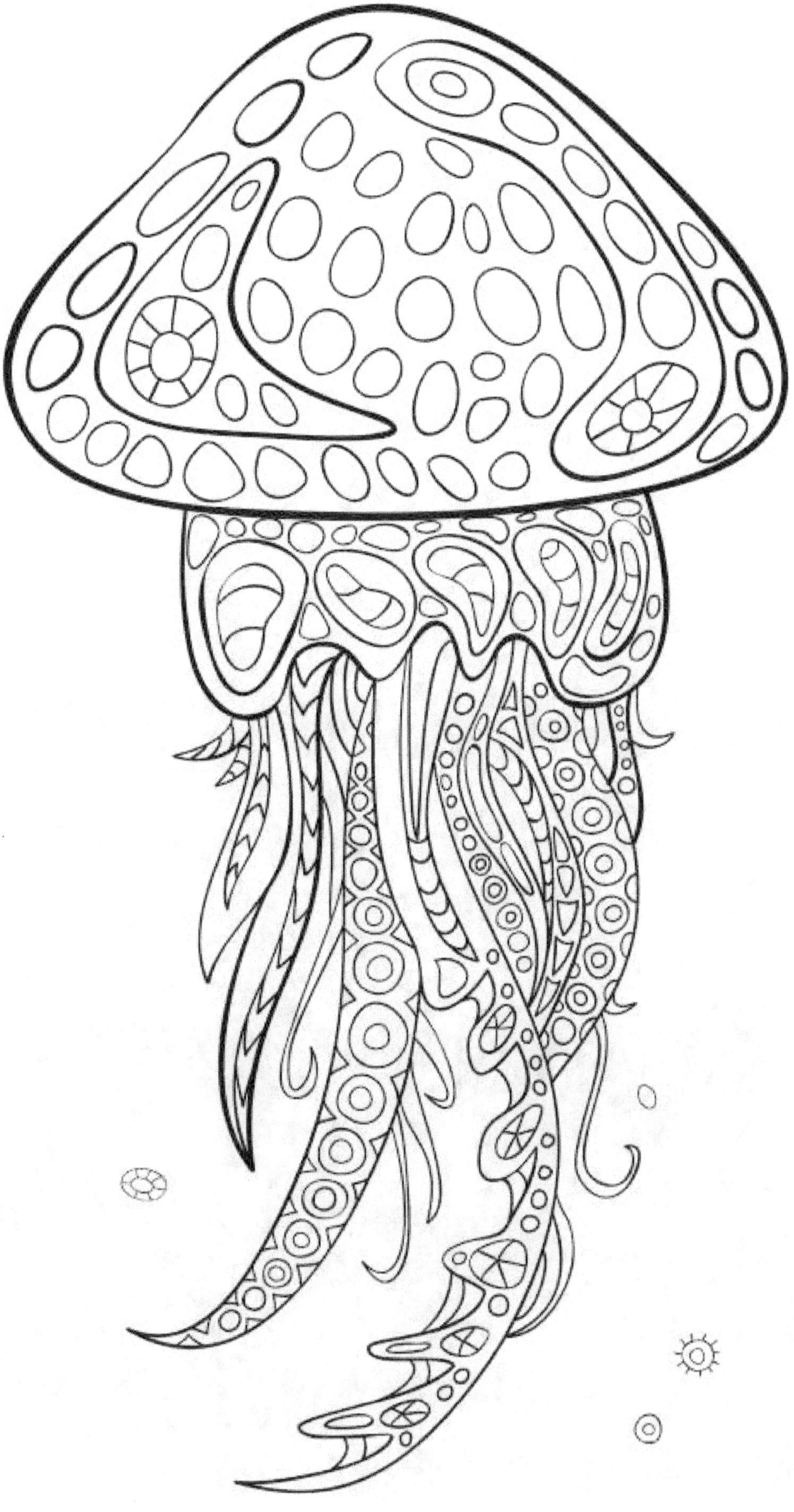

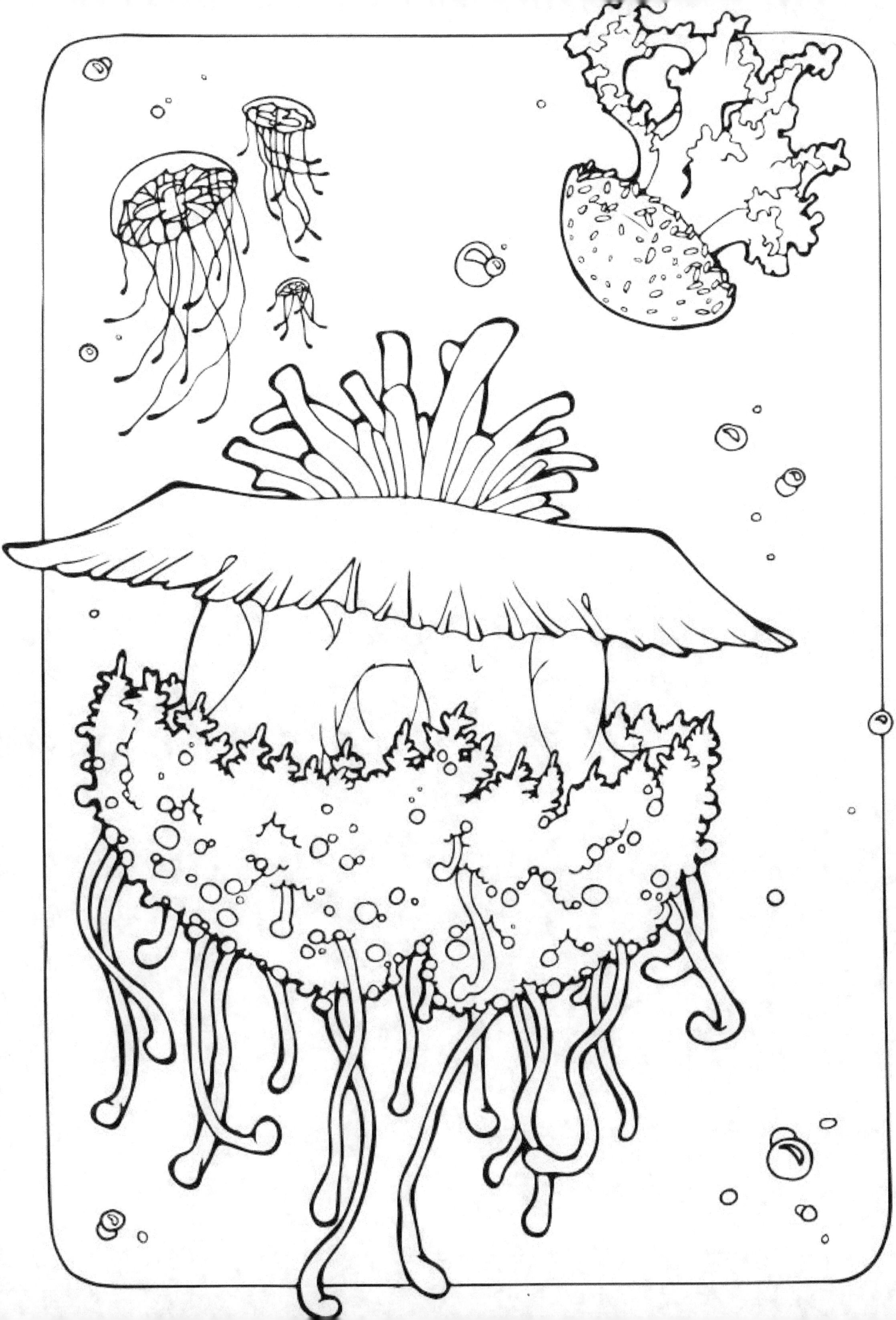

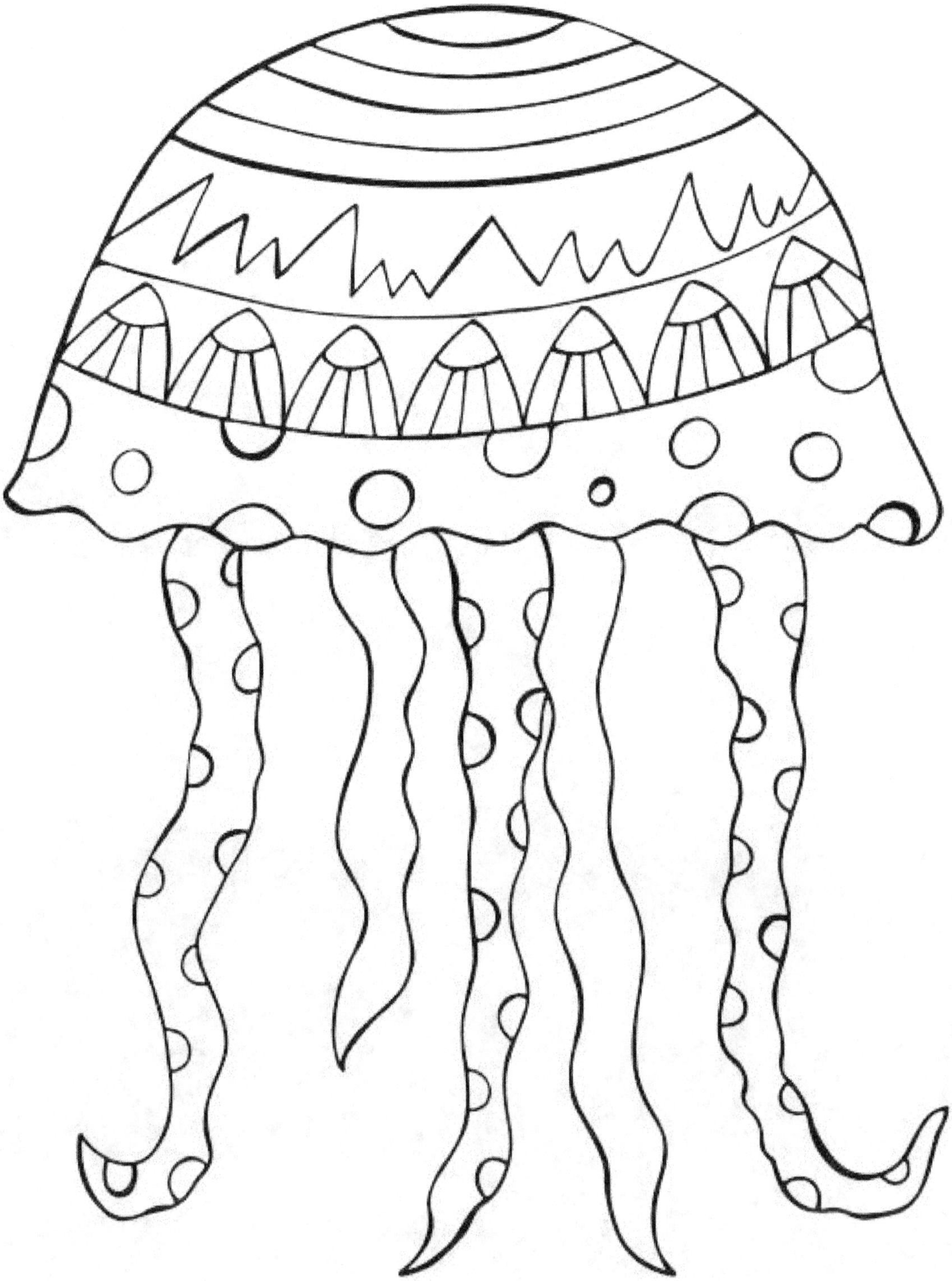

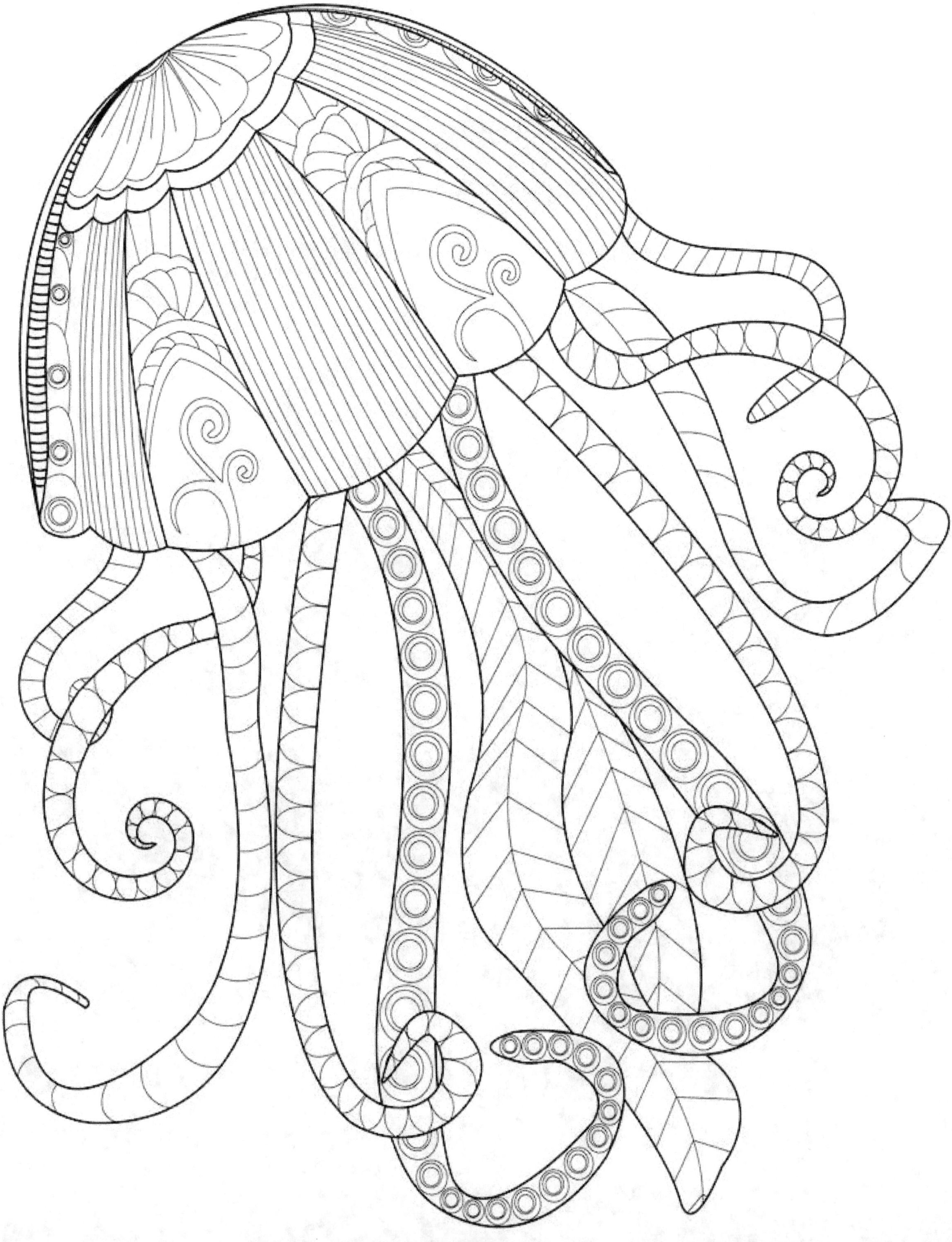

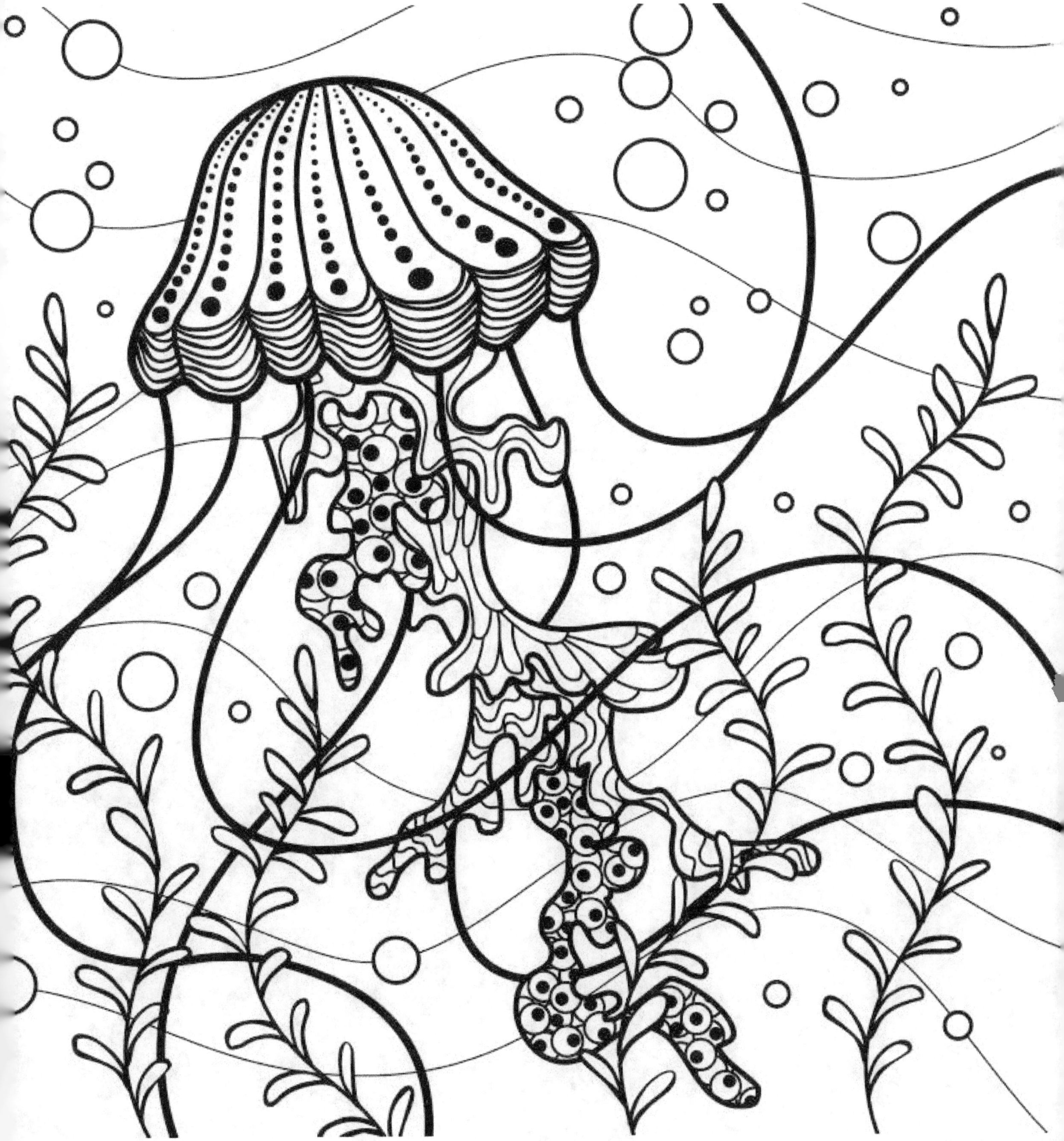

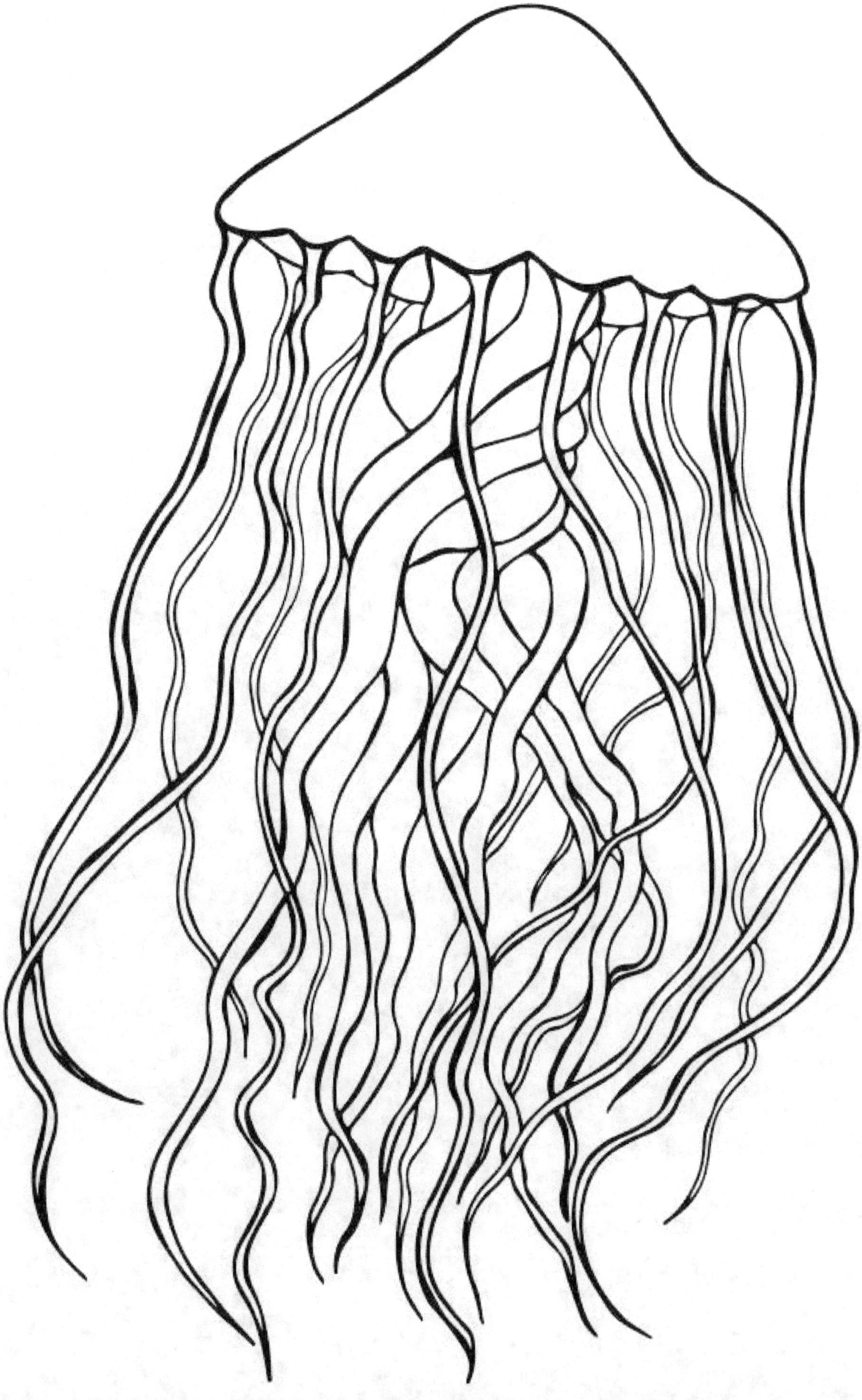

Free Surprise Bonus of Our Whales and Sea Turtles. Enjoy!

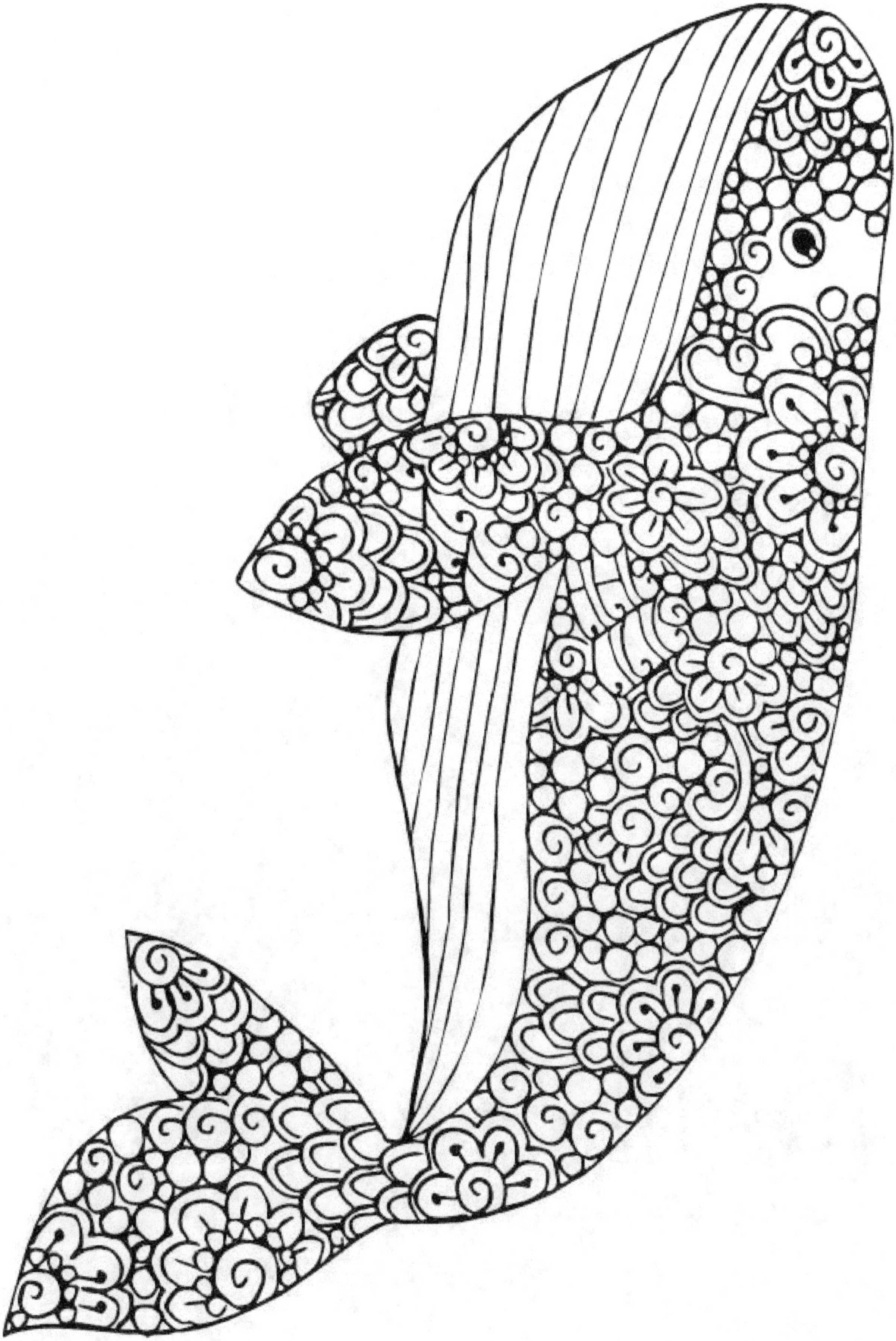

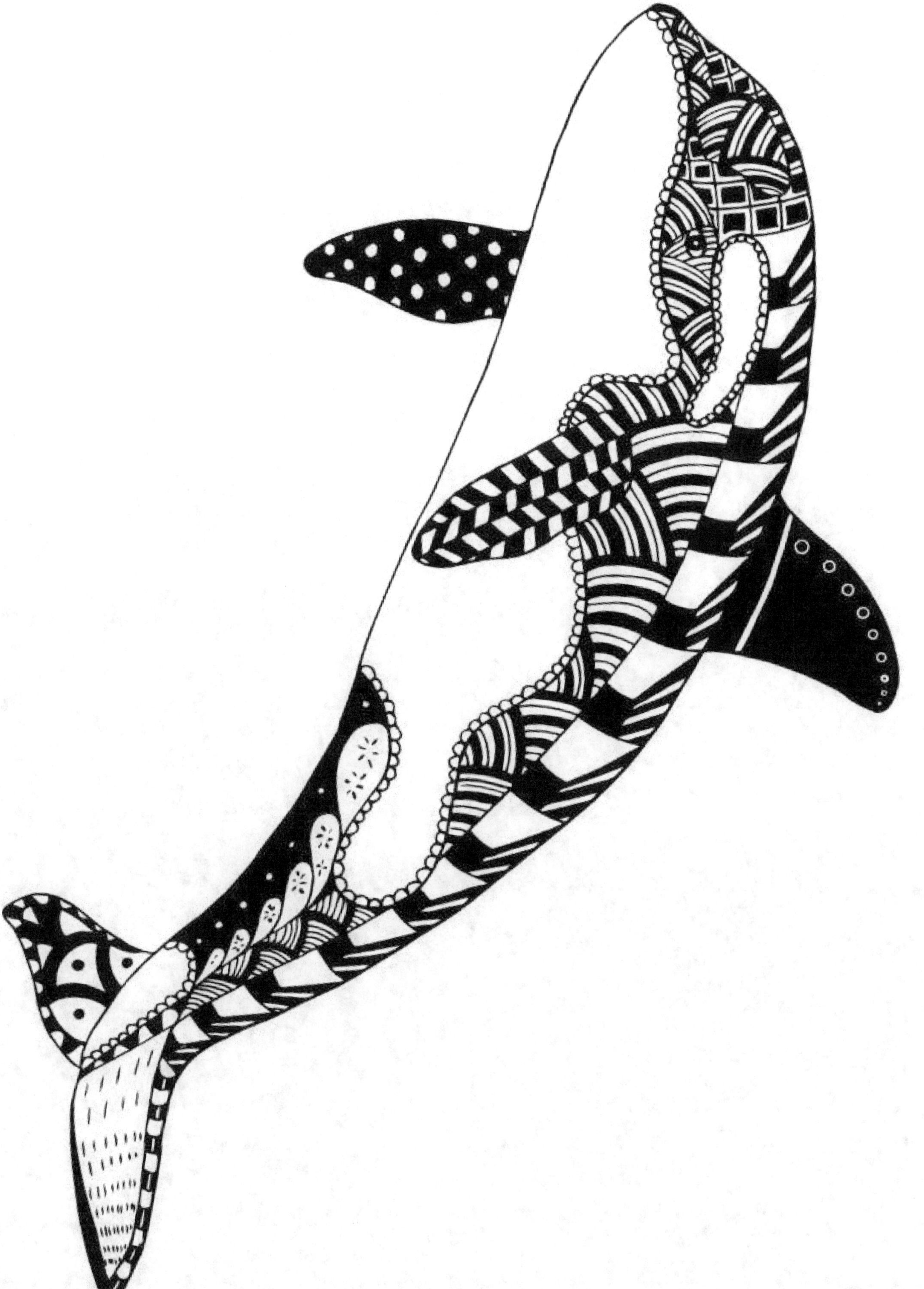

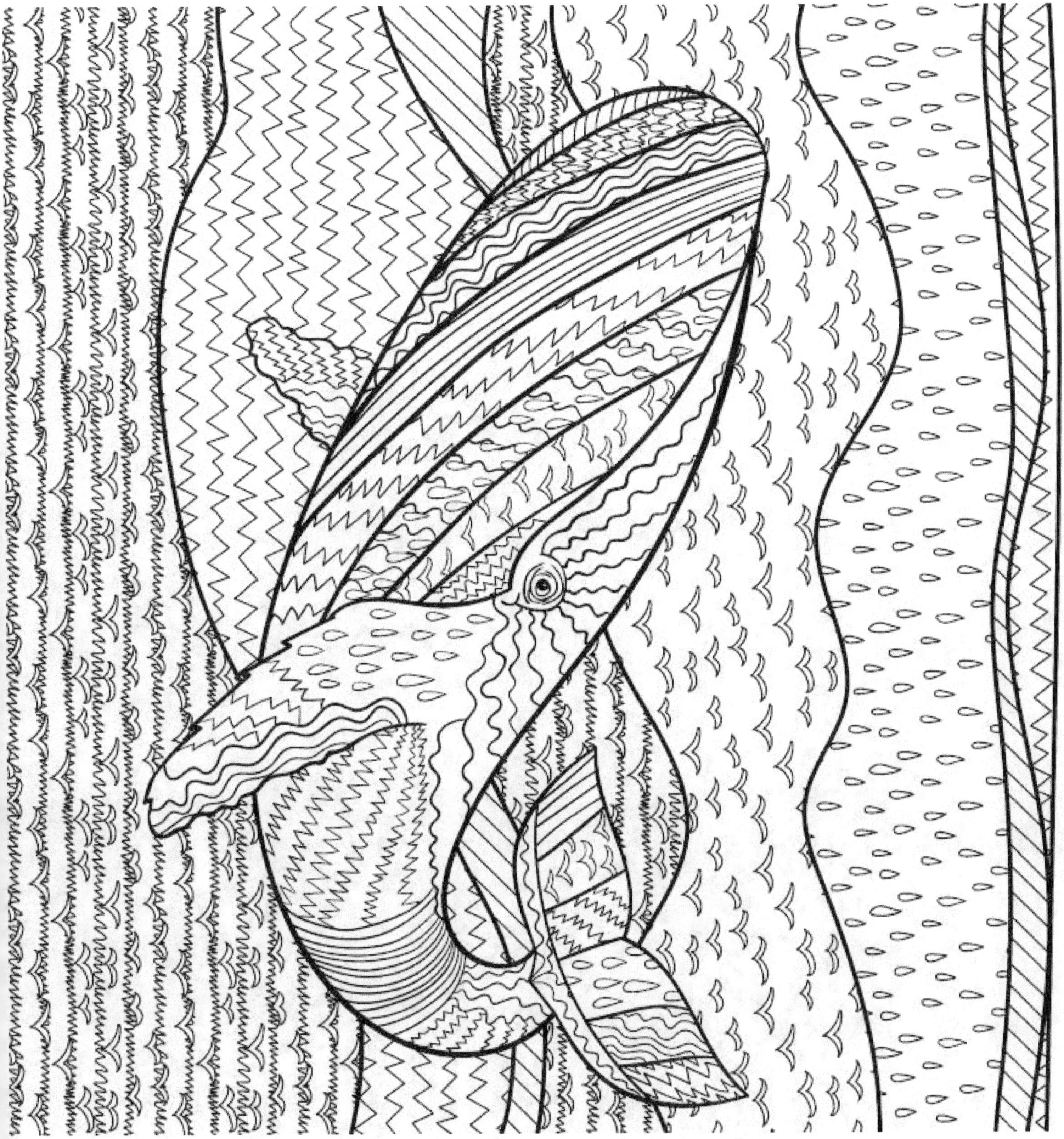

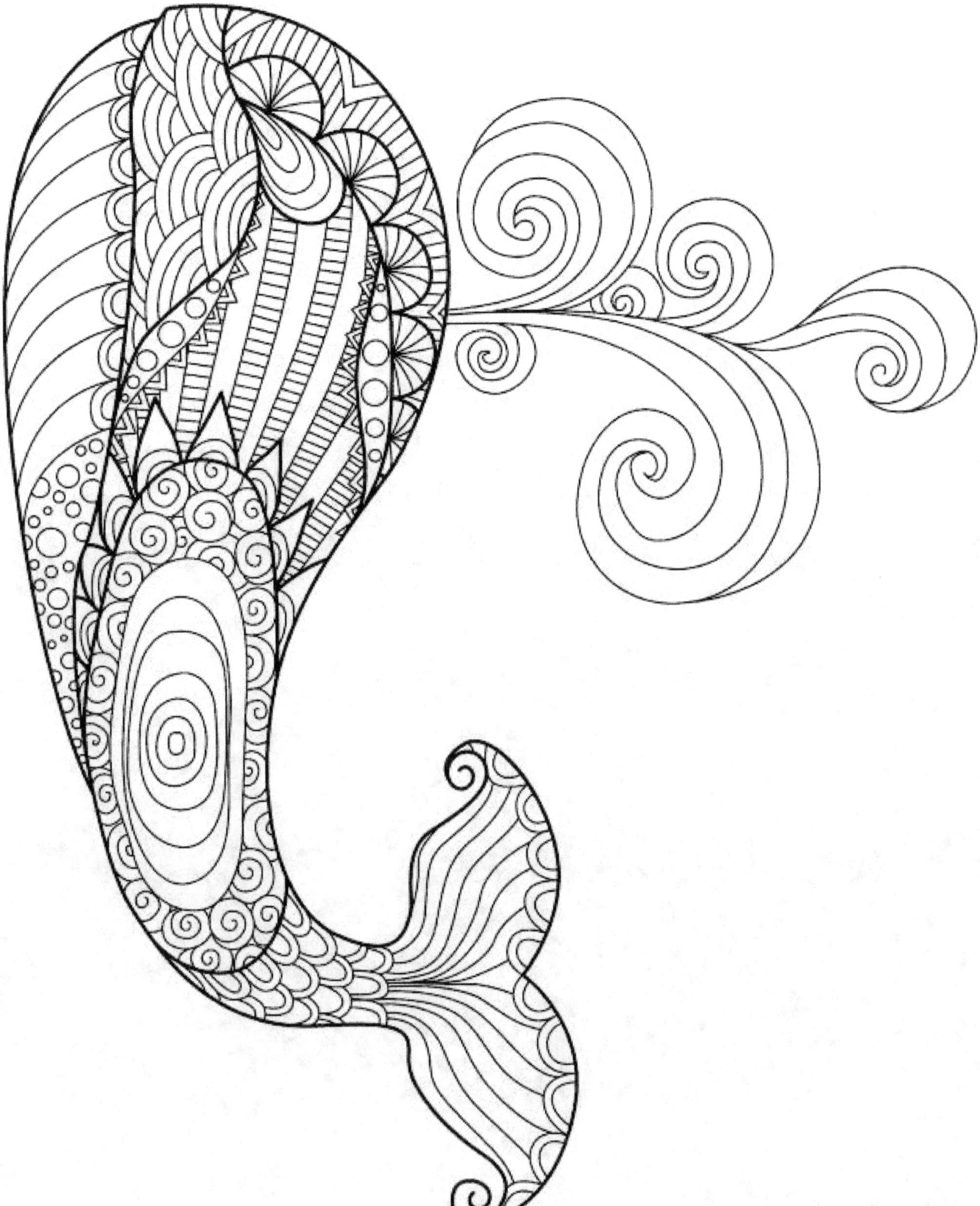

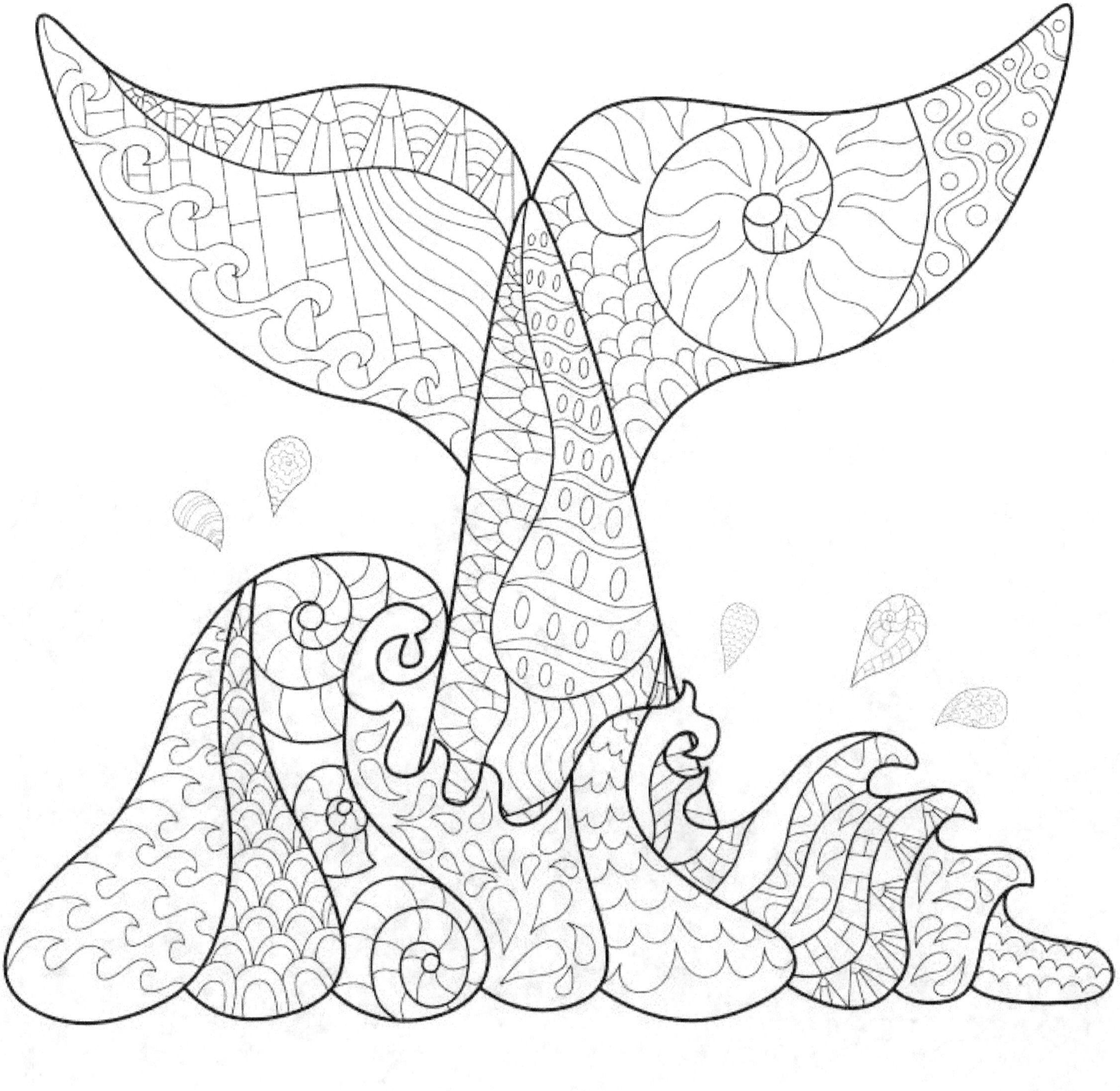

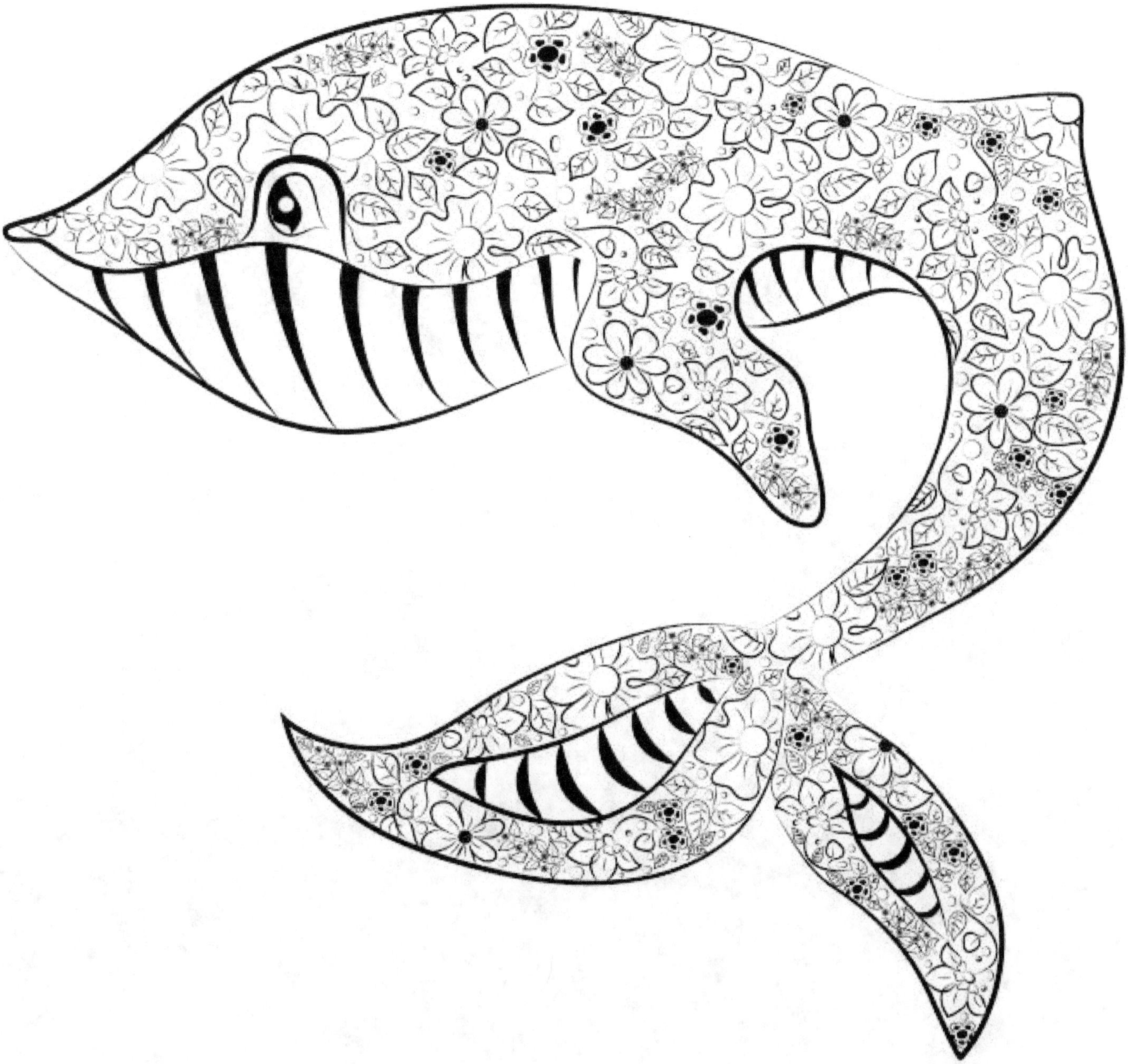

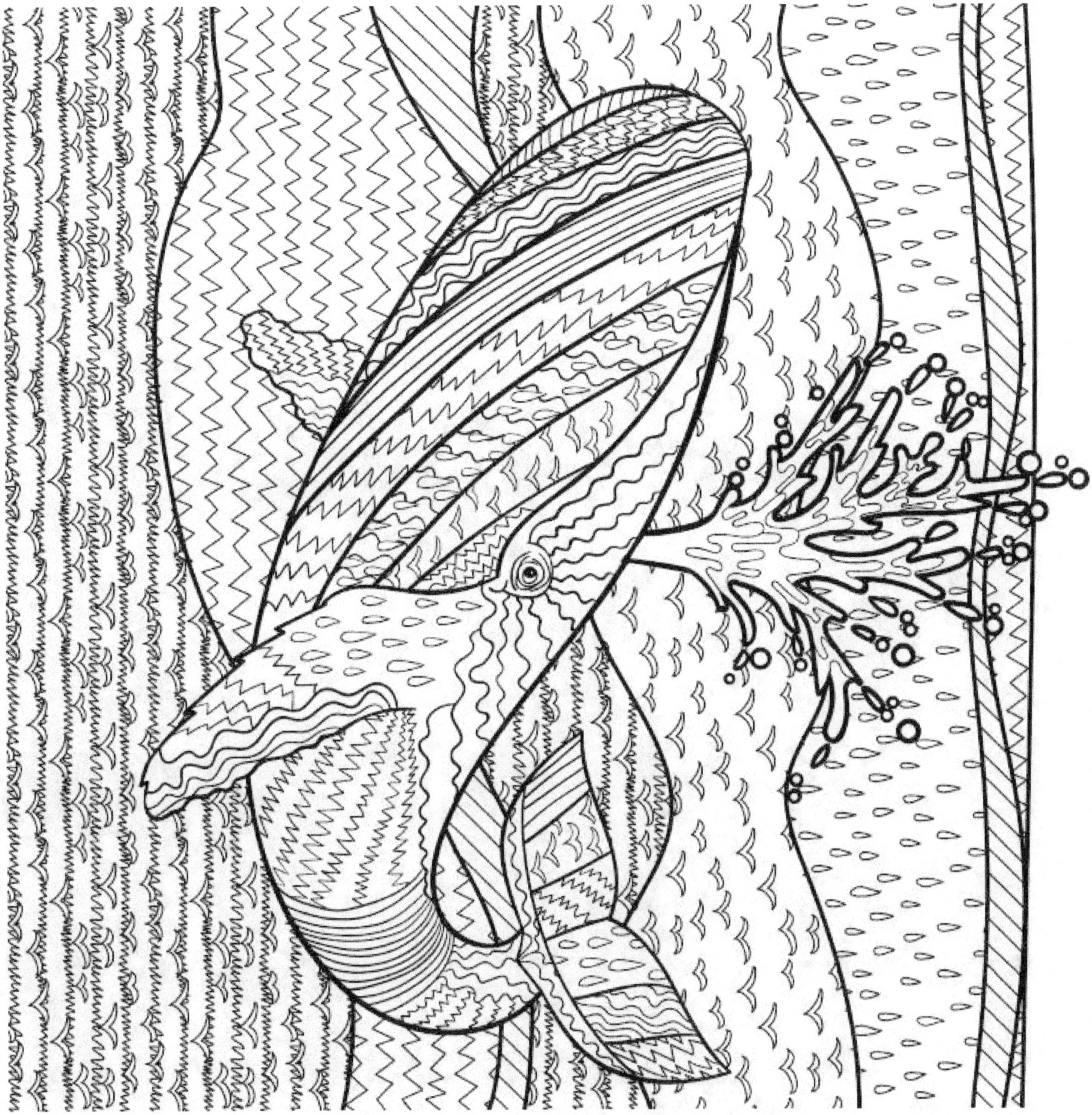

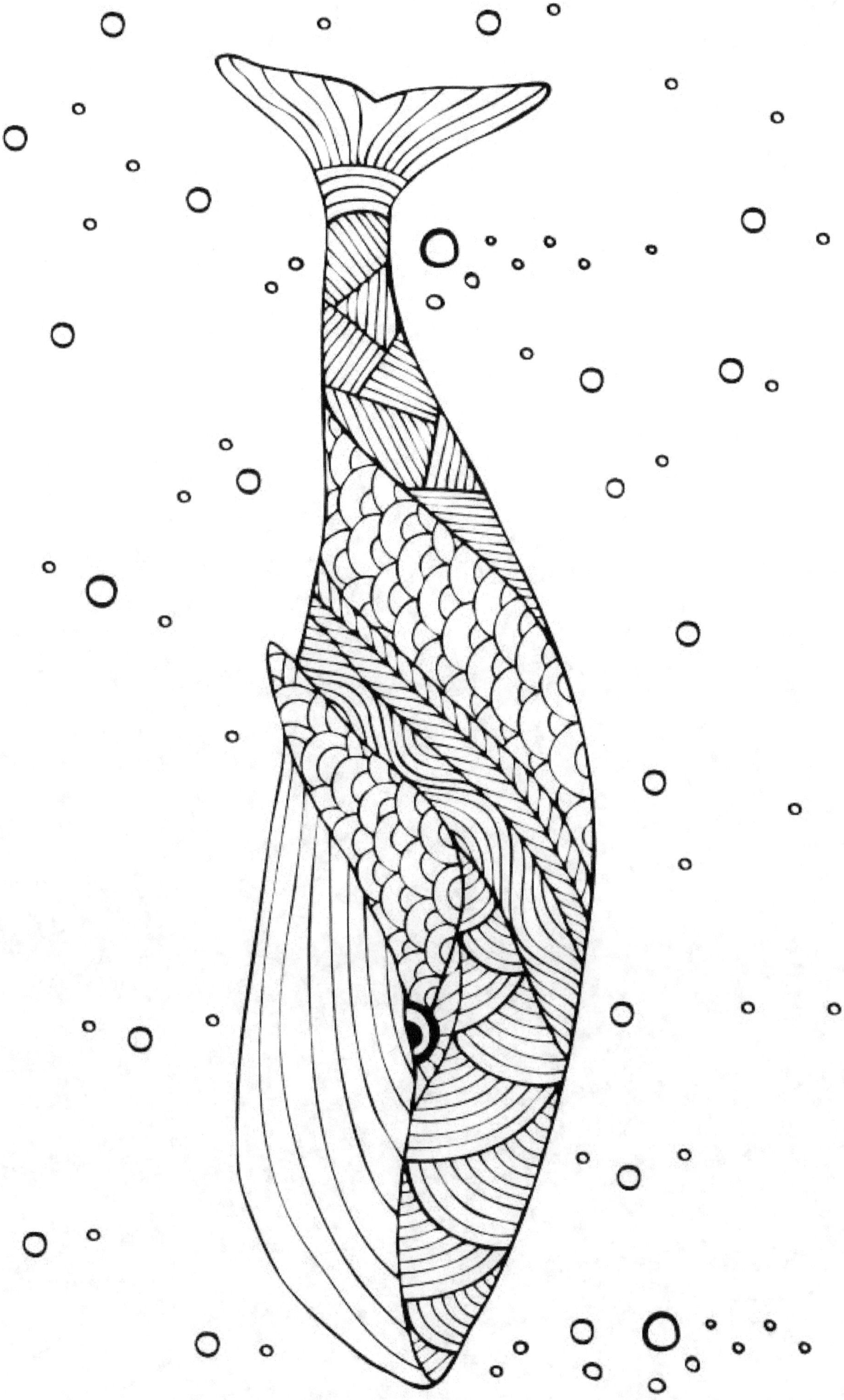

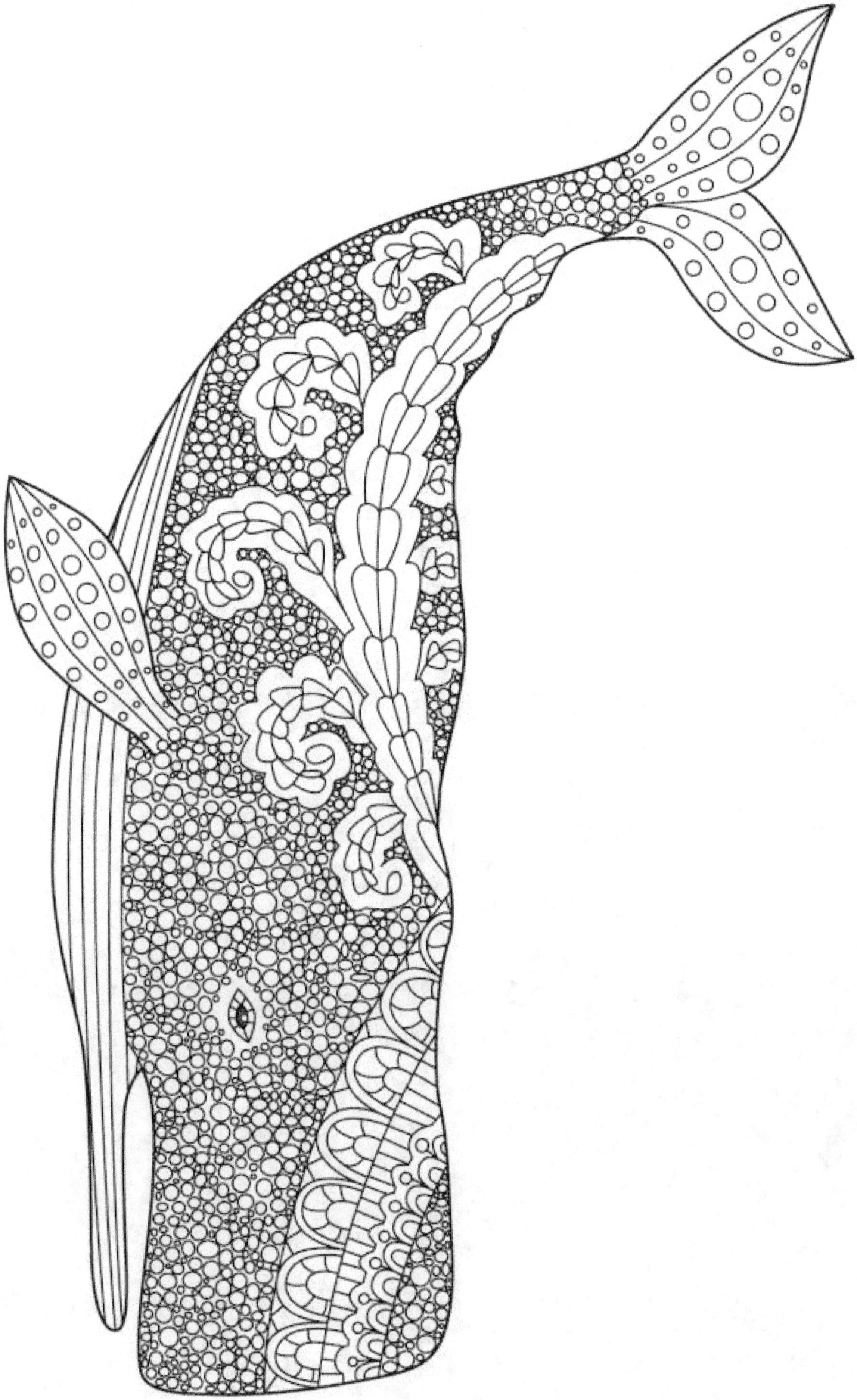

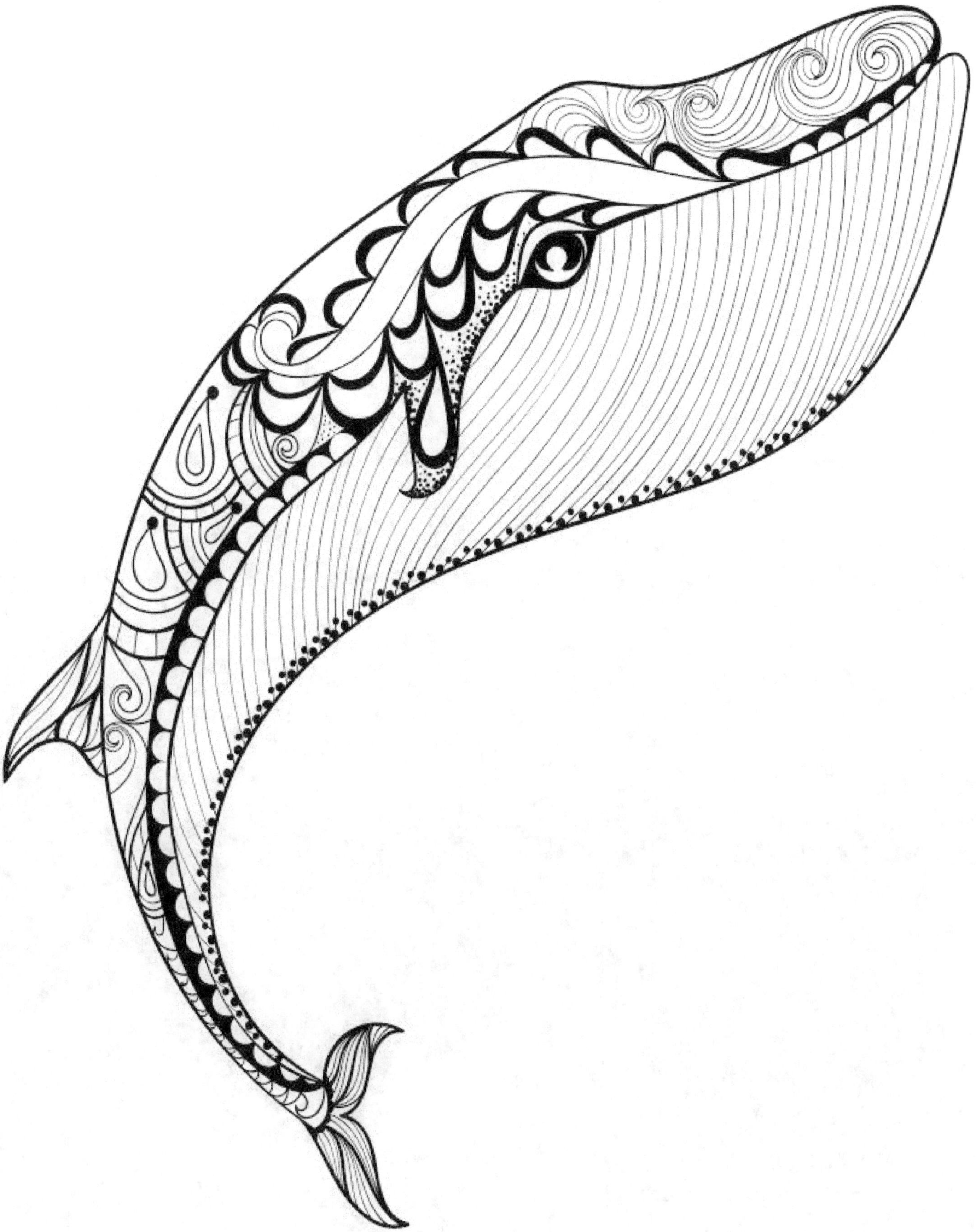

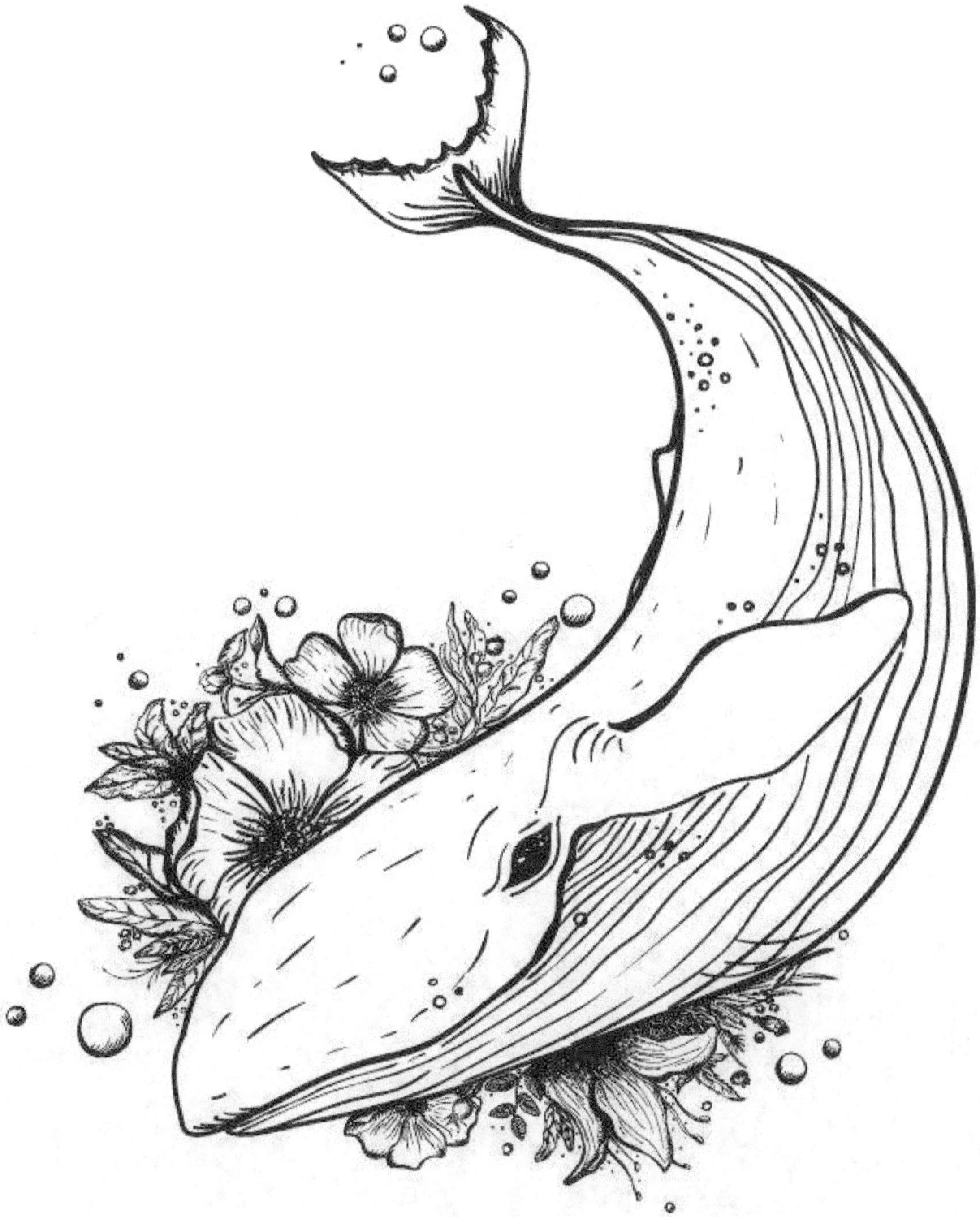

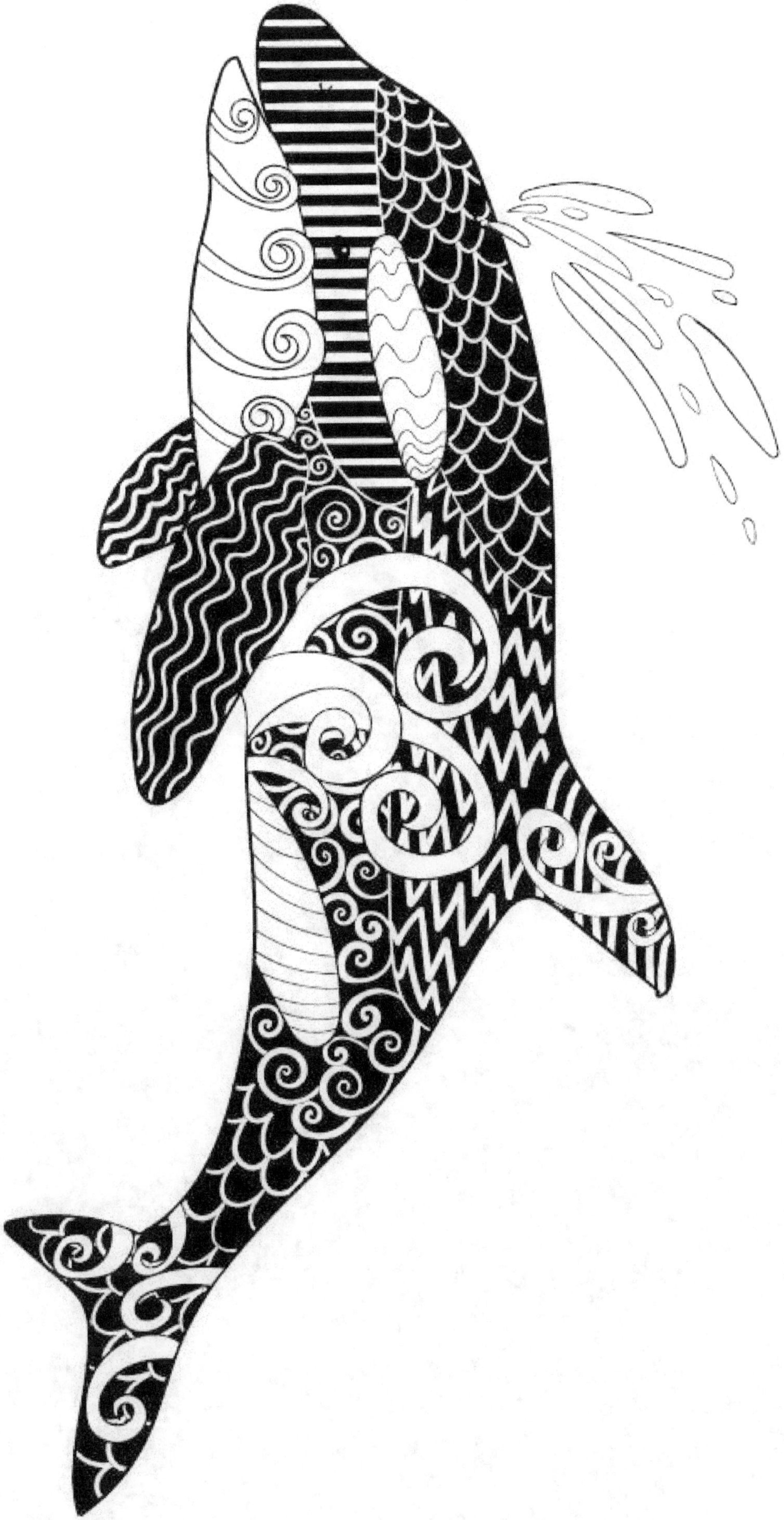

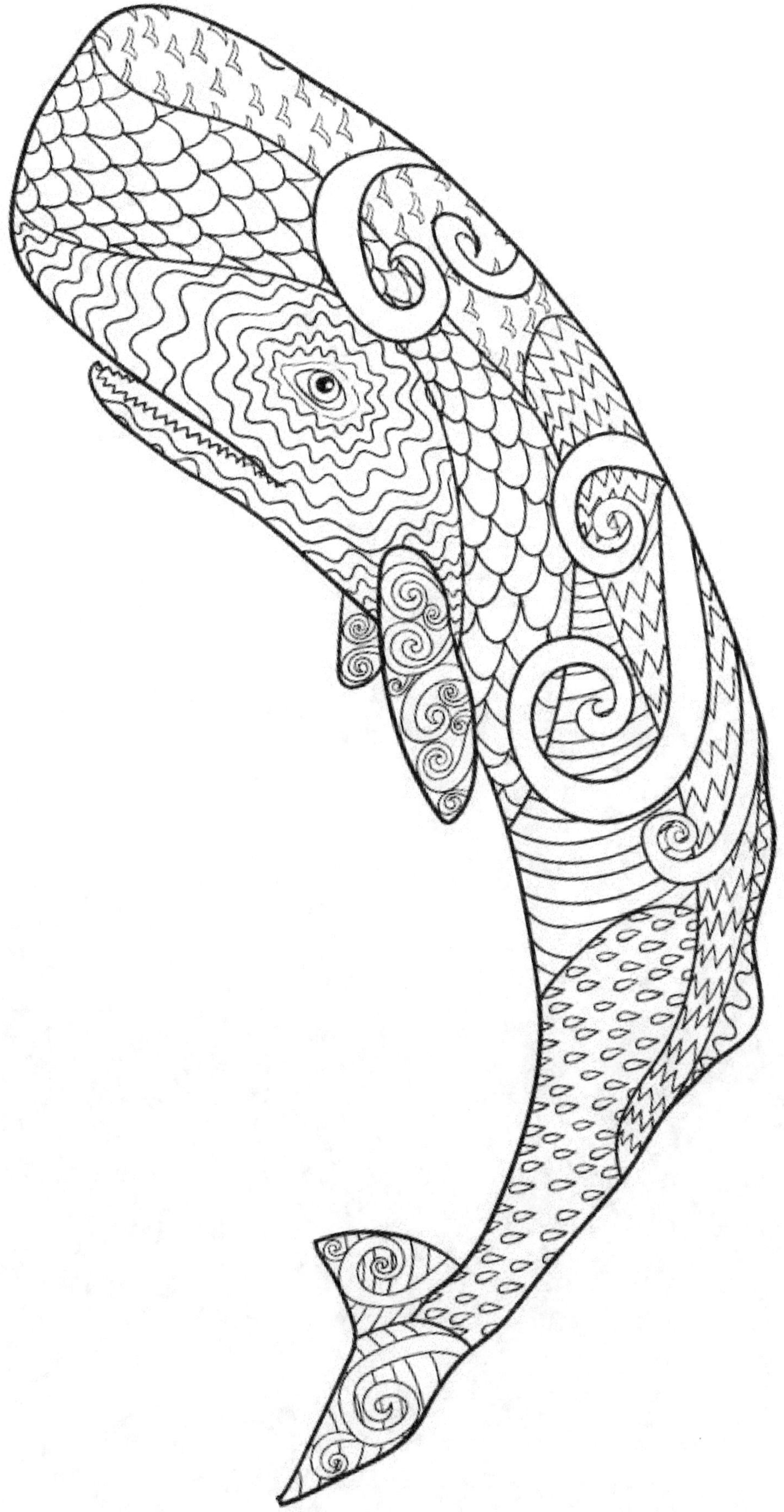

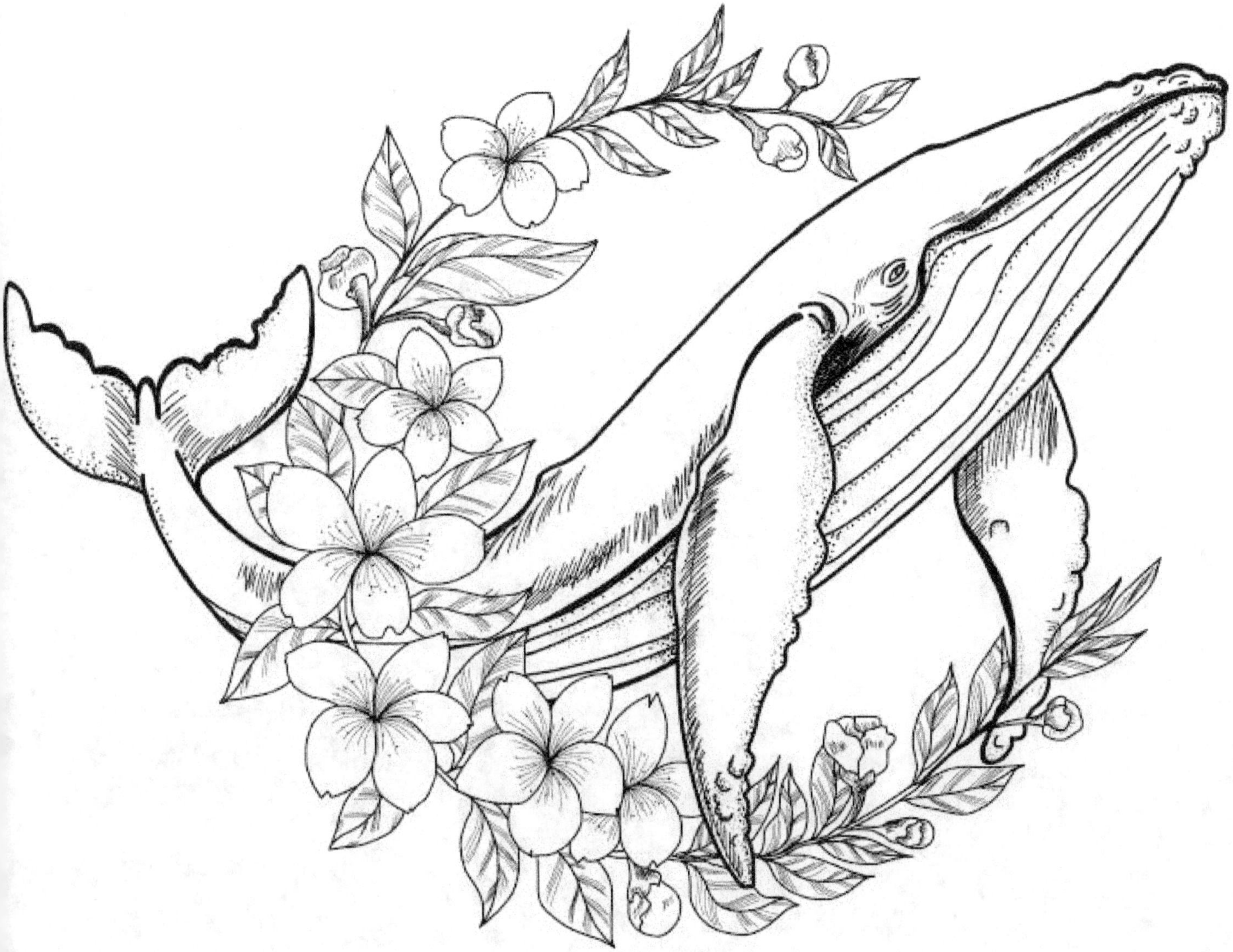

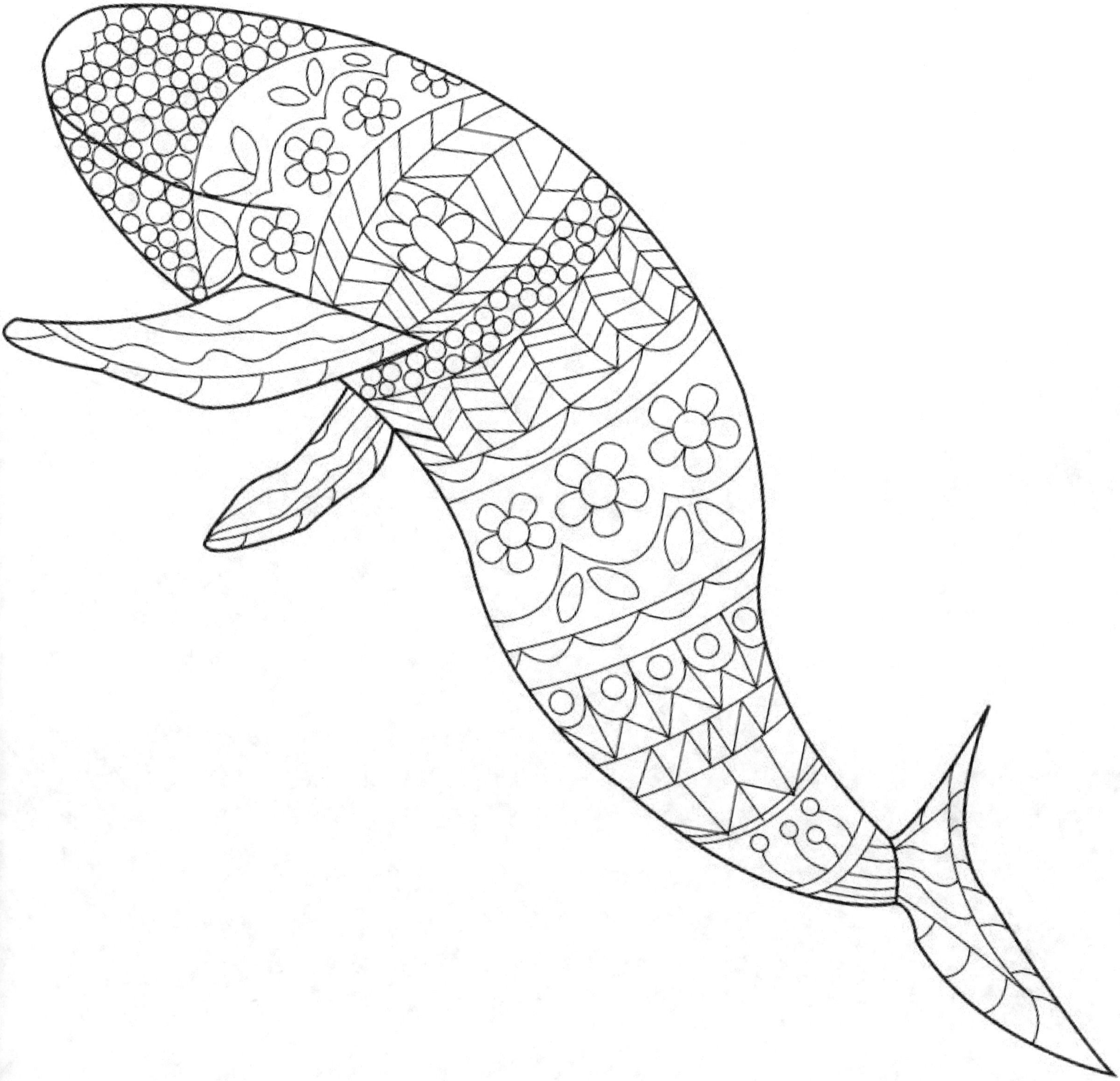

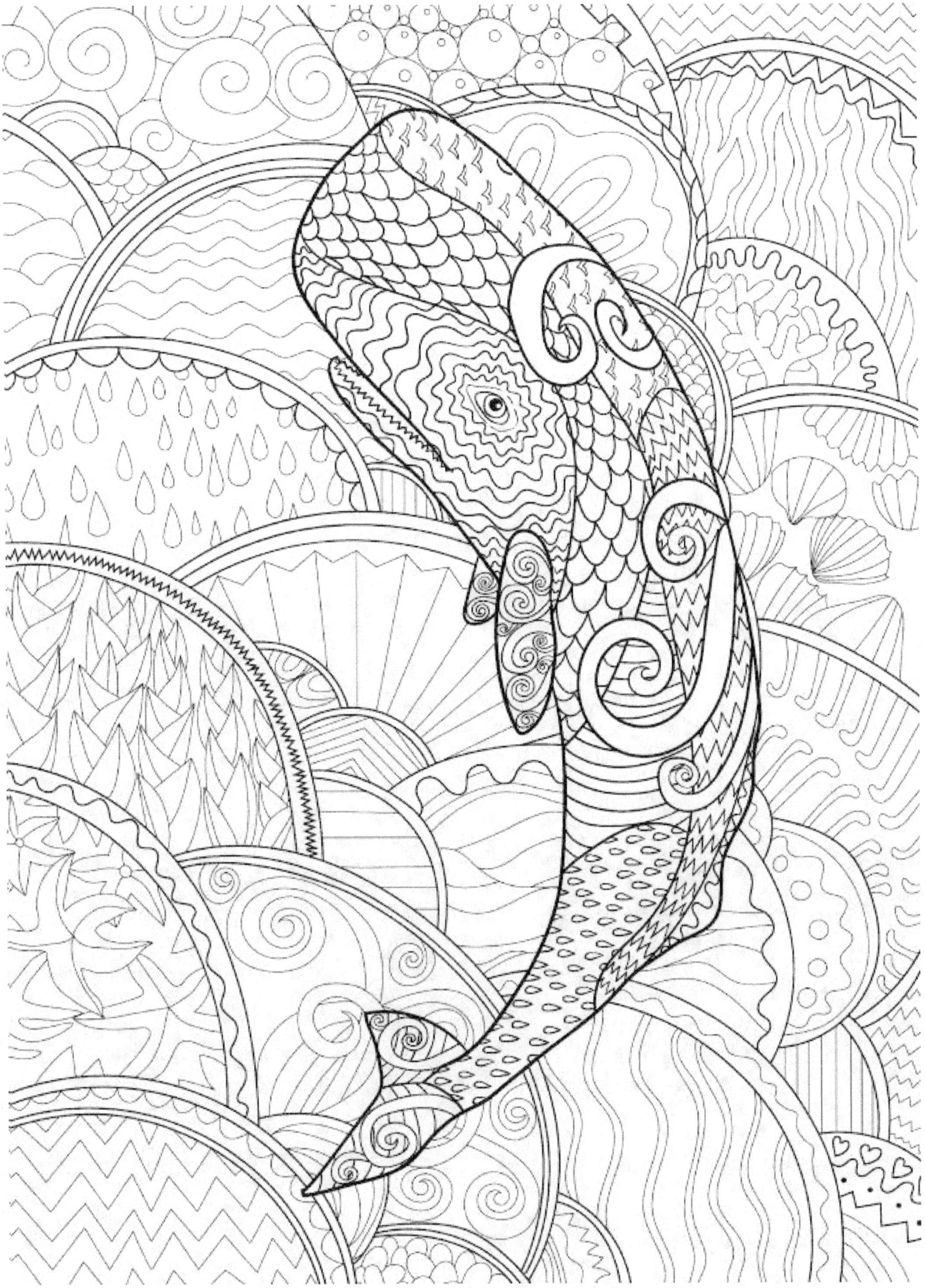

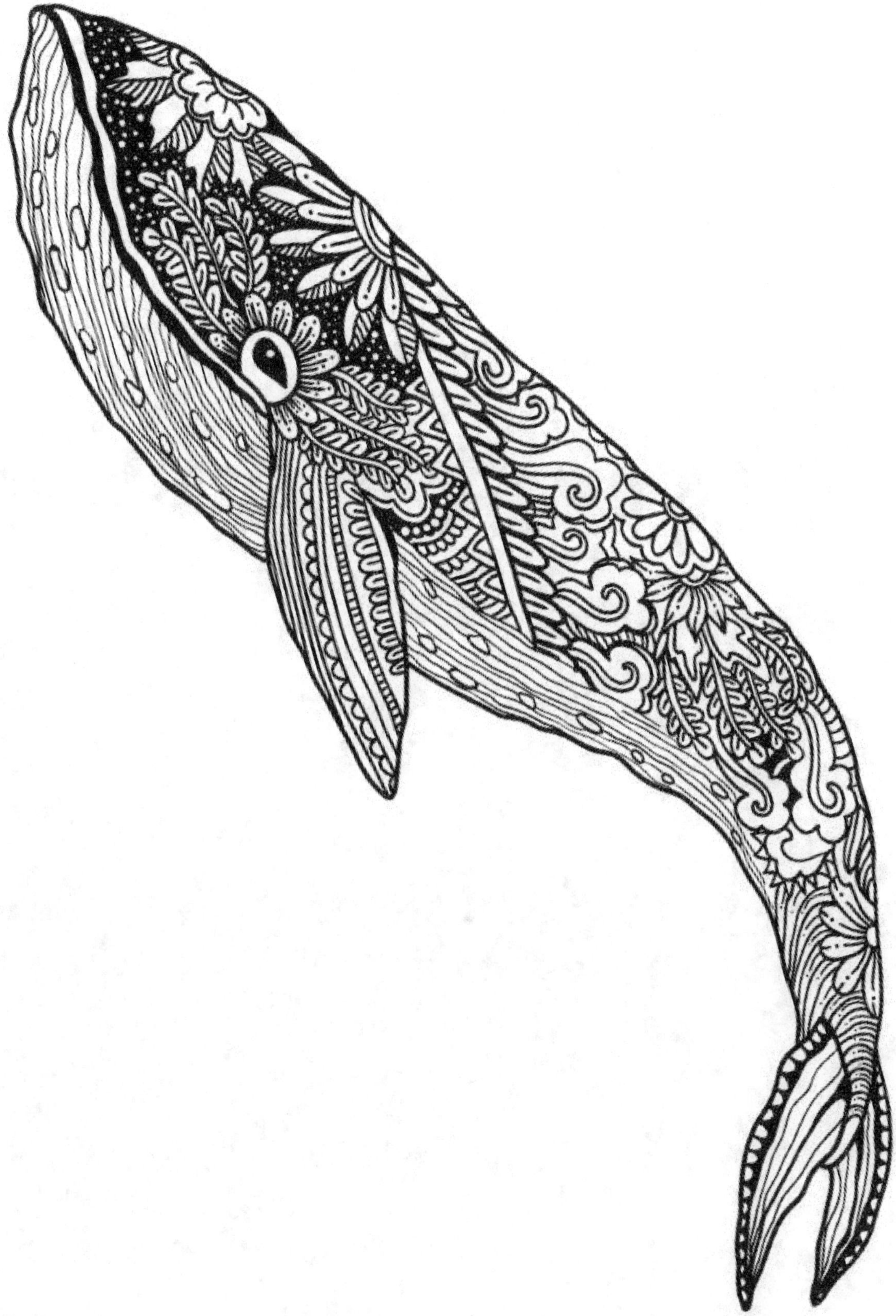

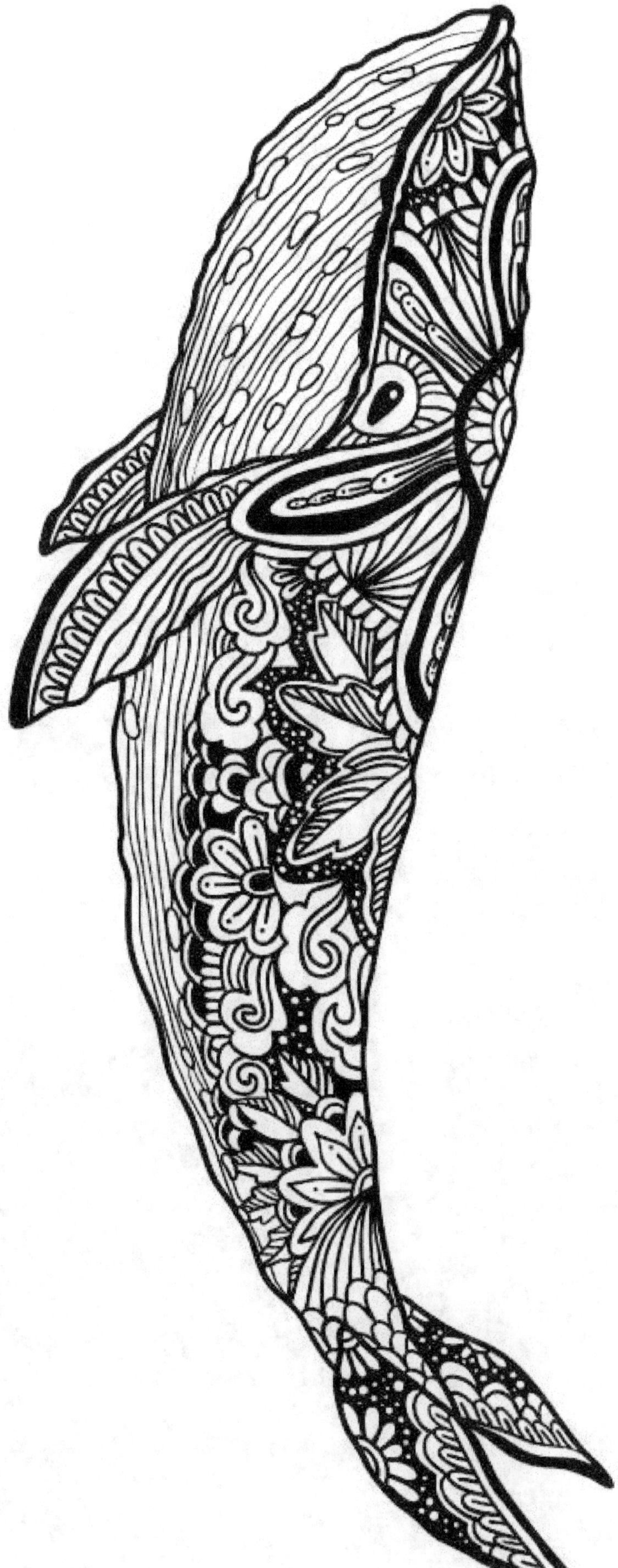

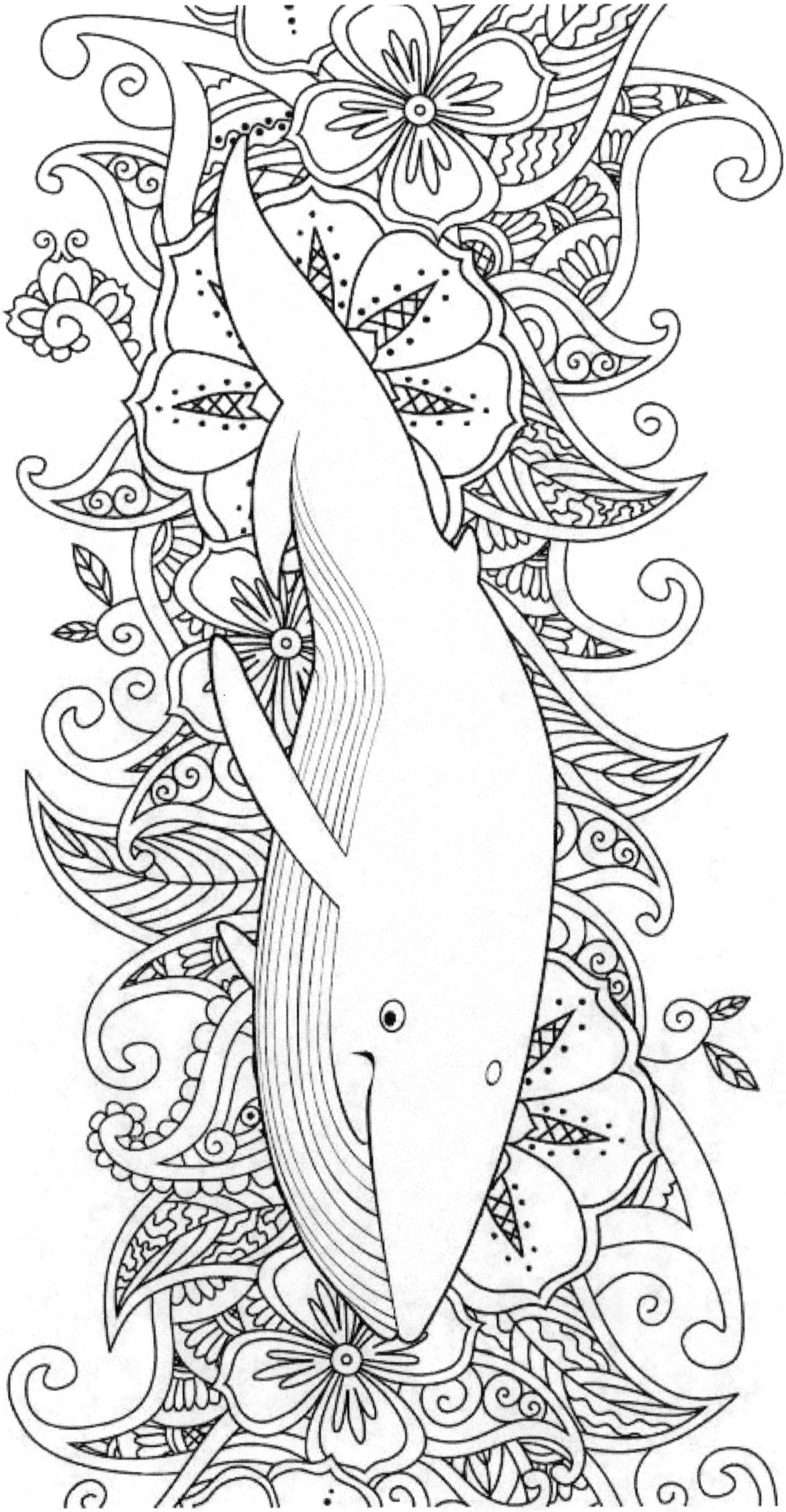

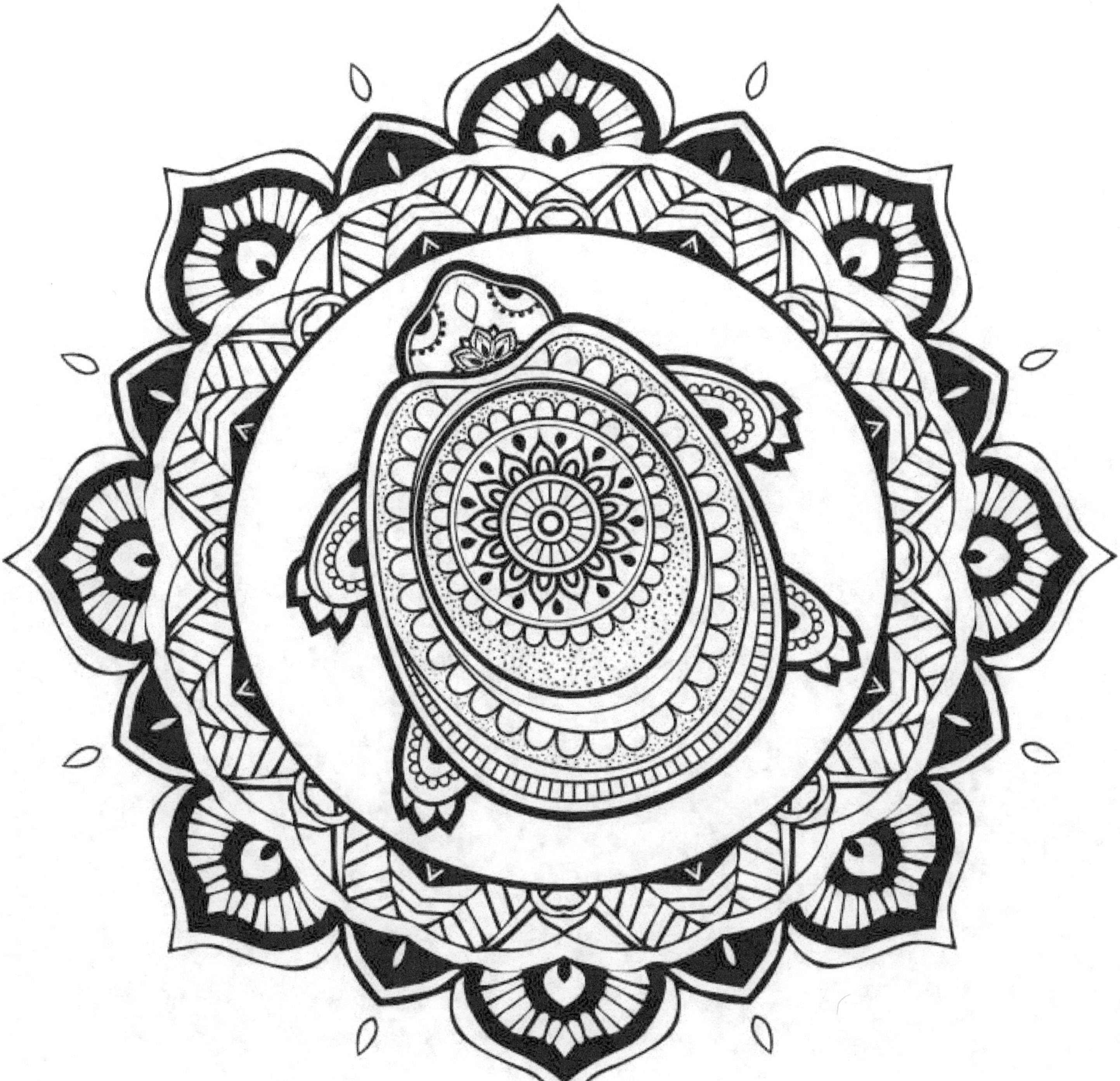

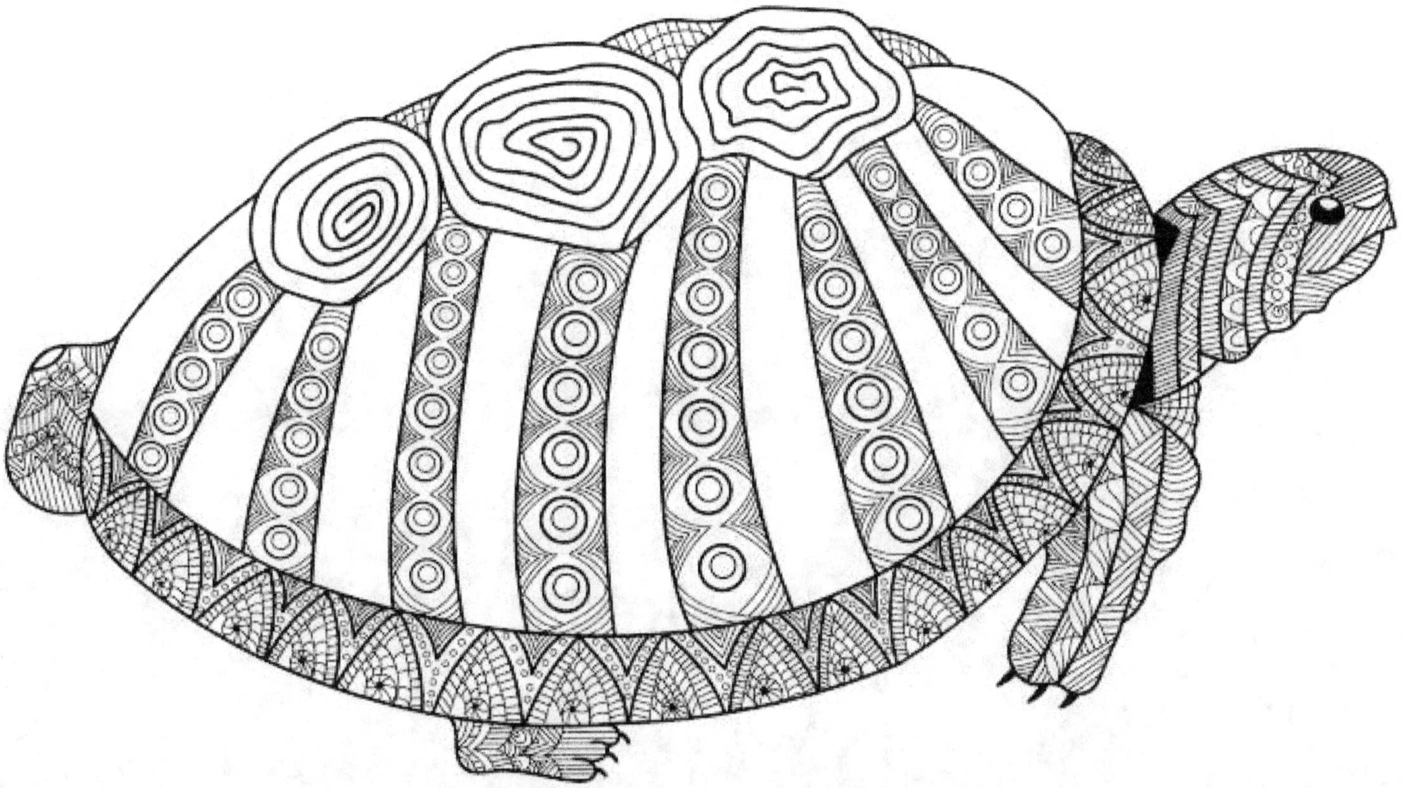

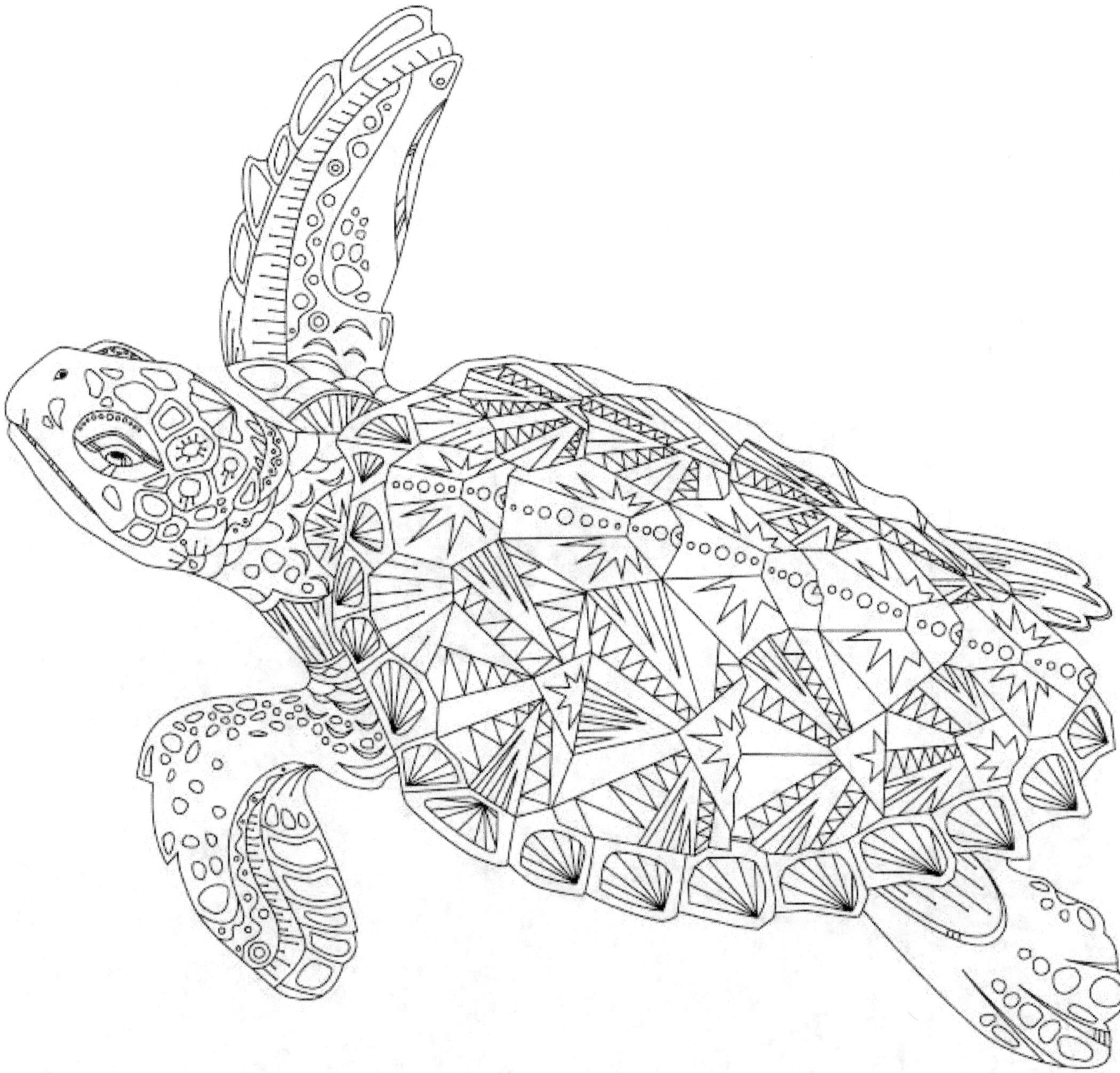

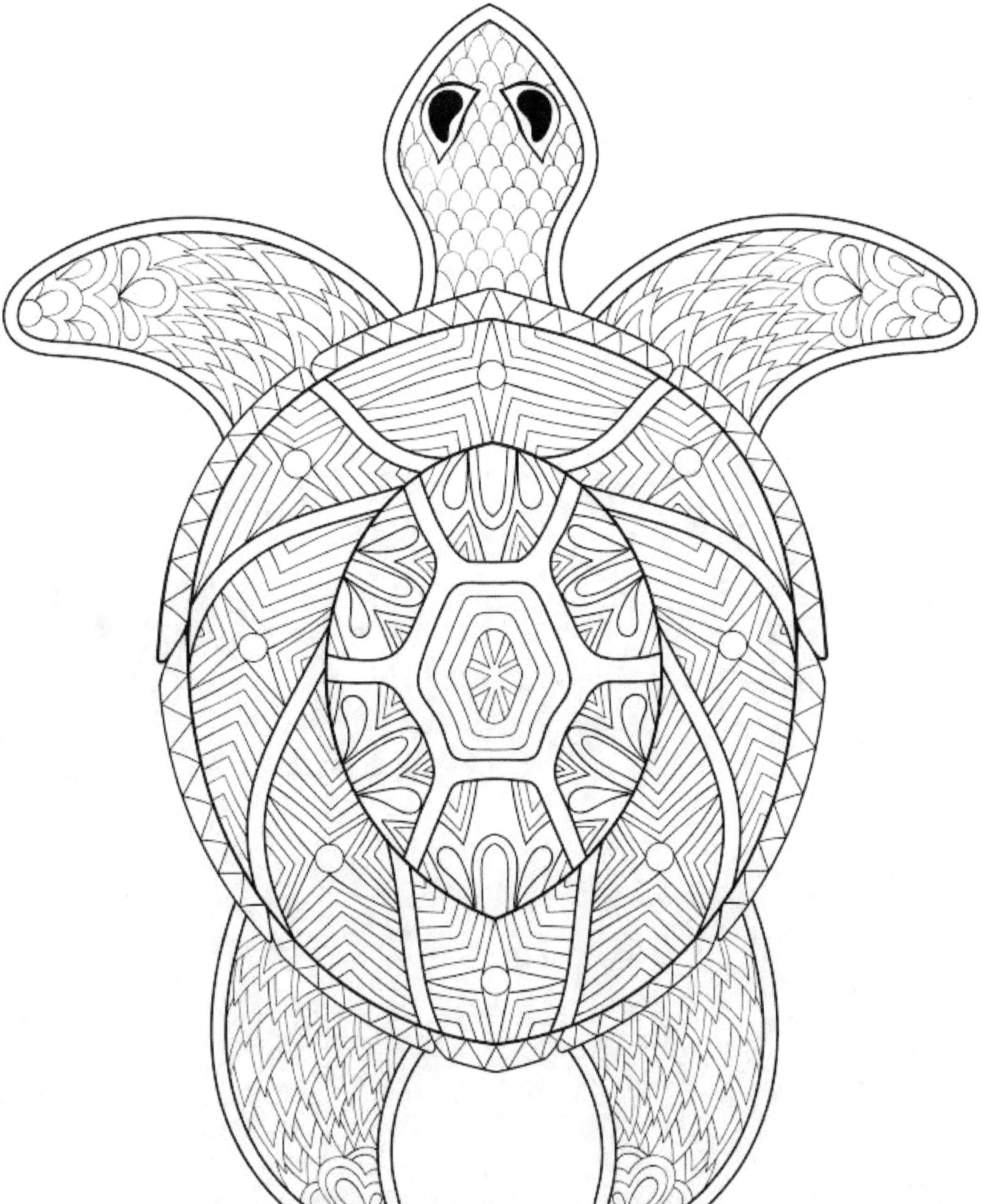

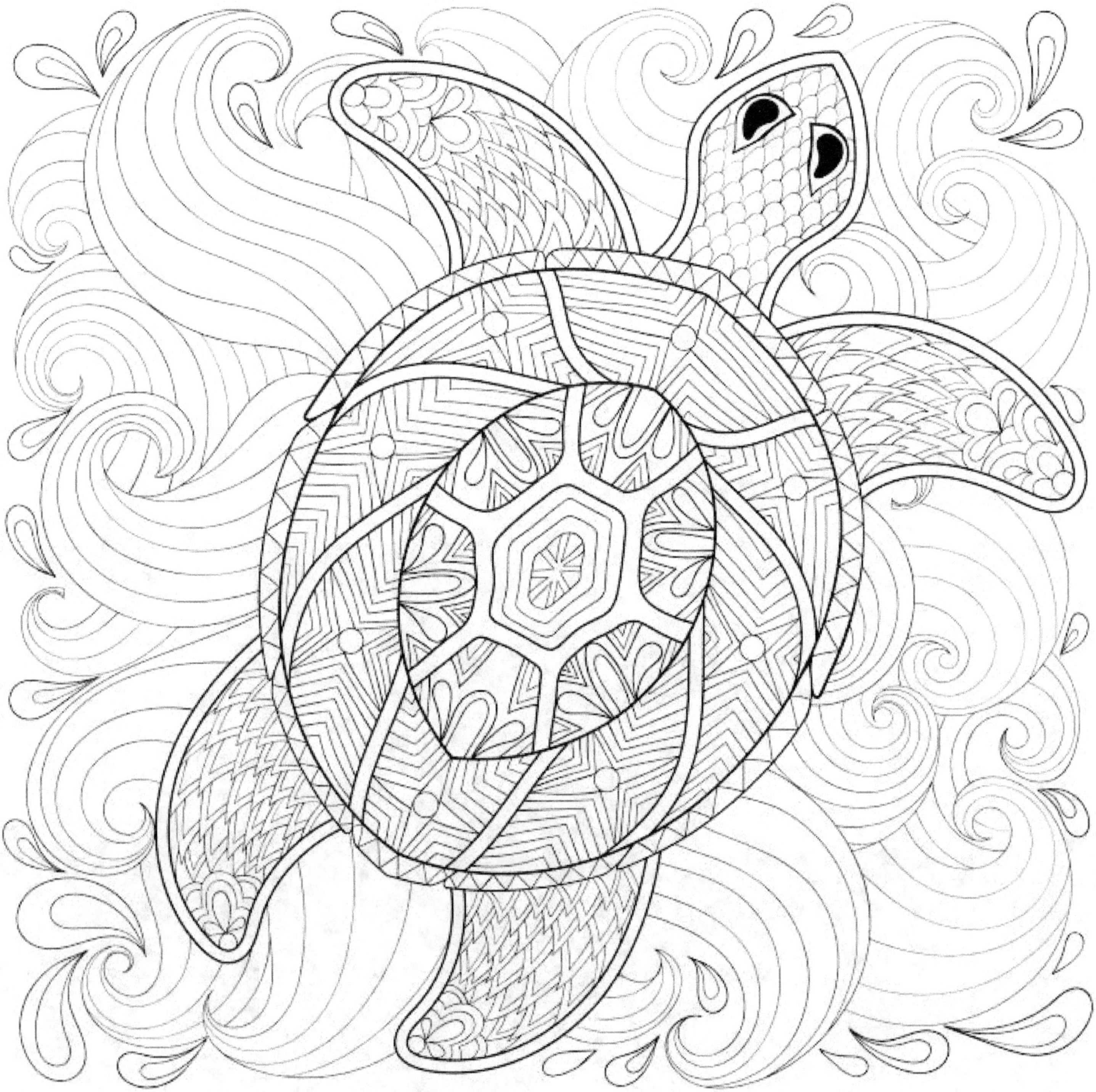

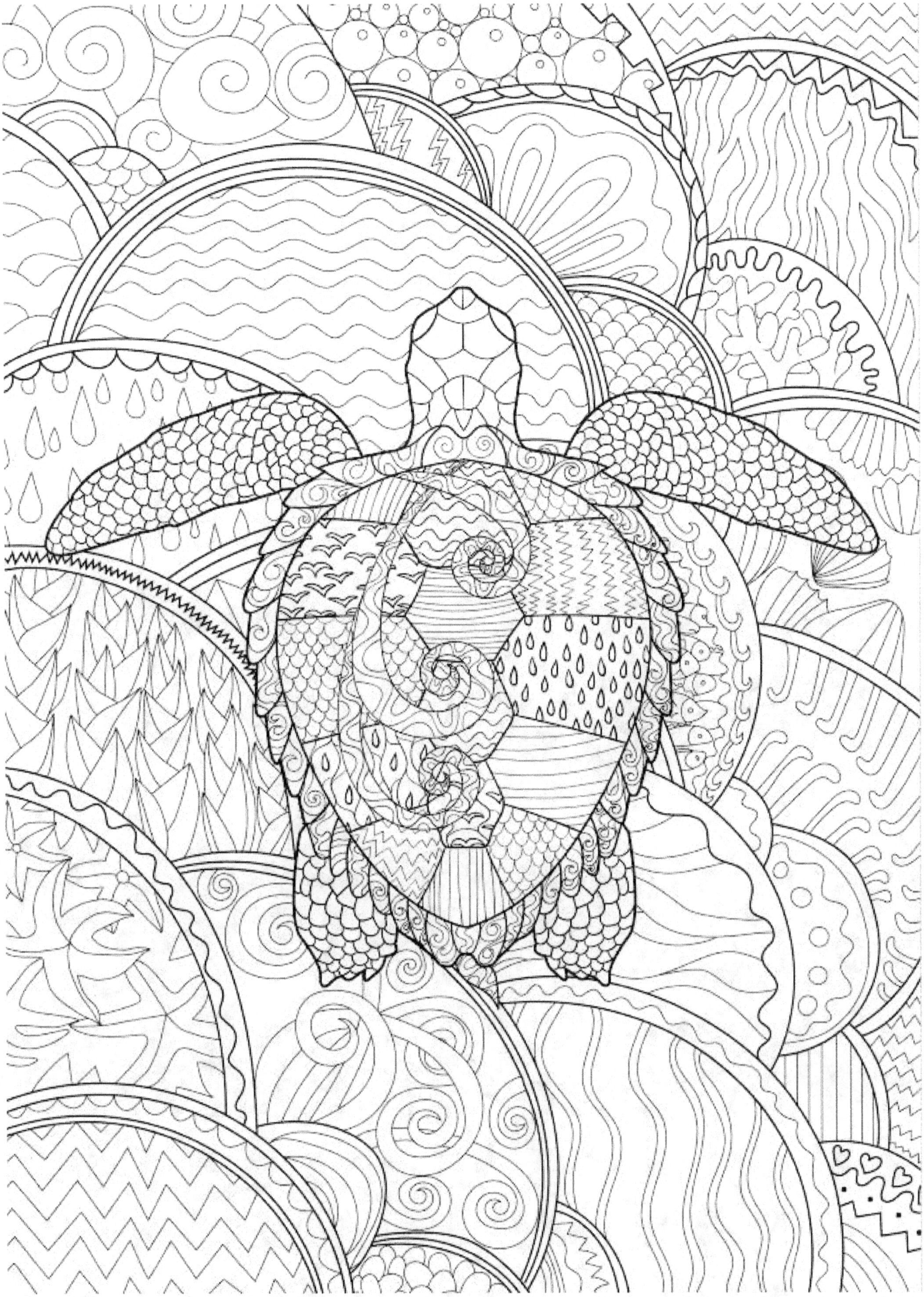

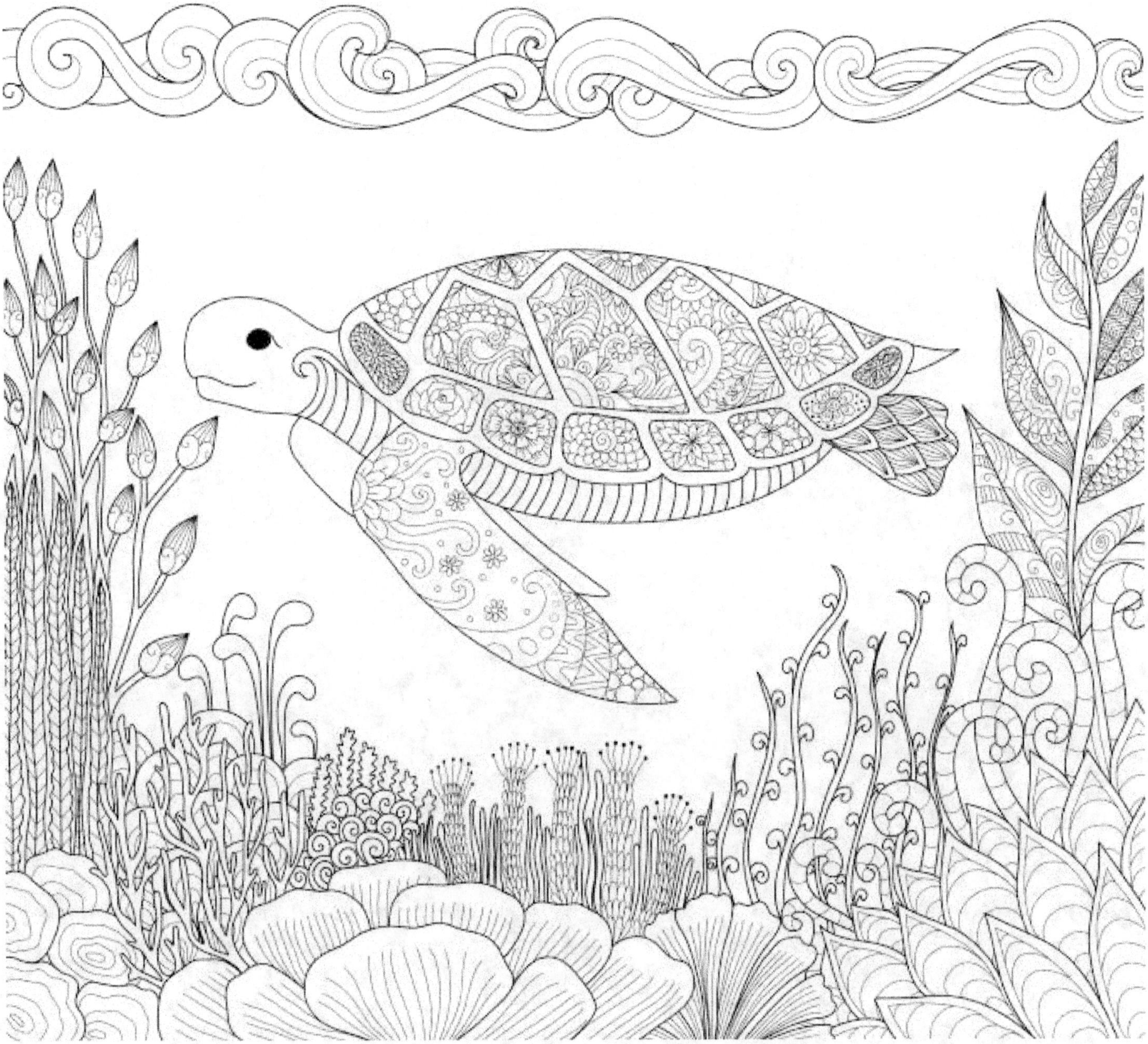

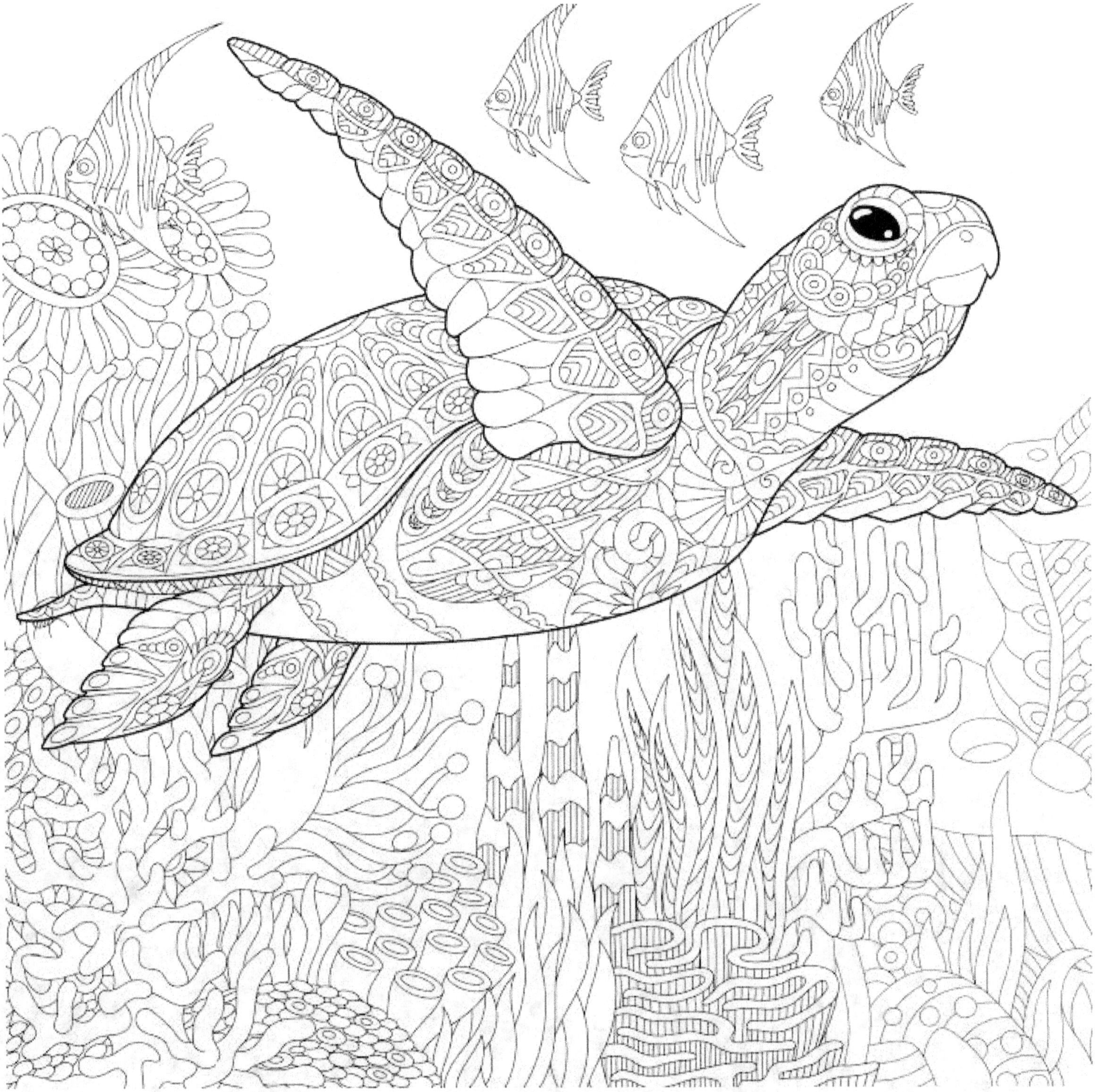

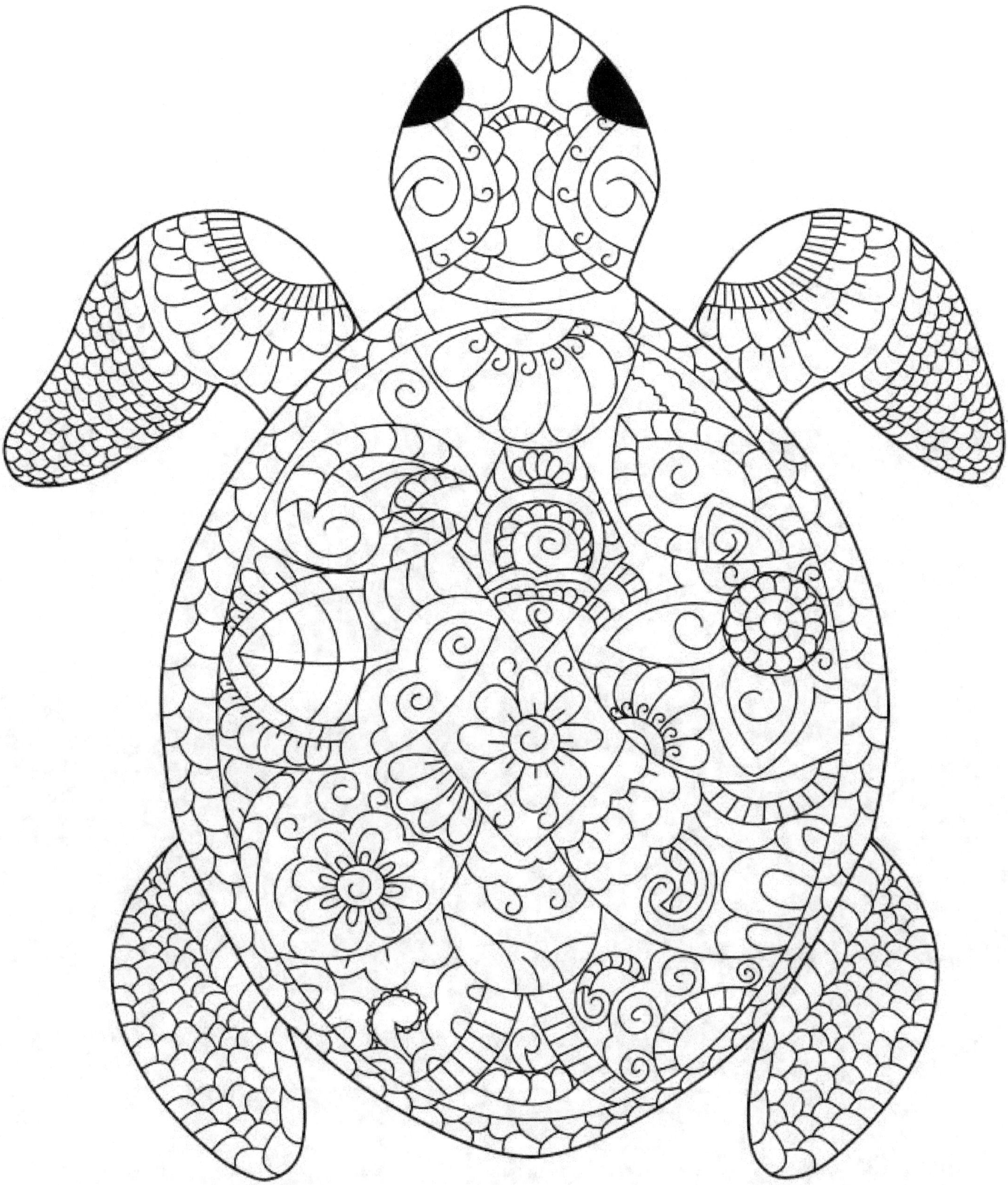

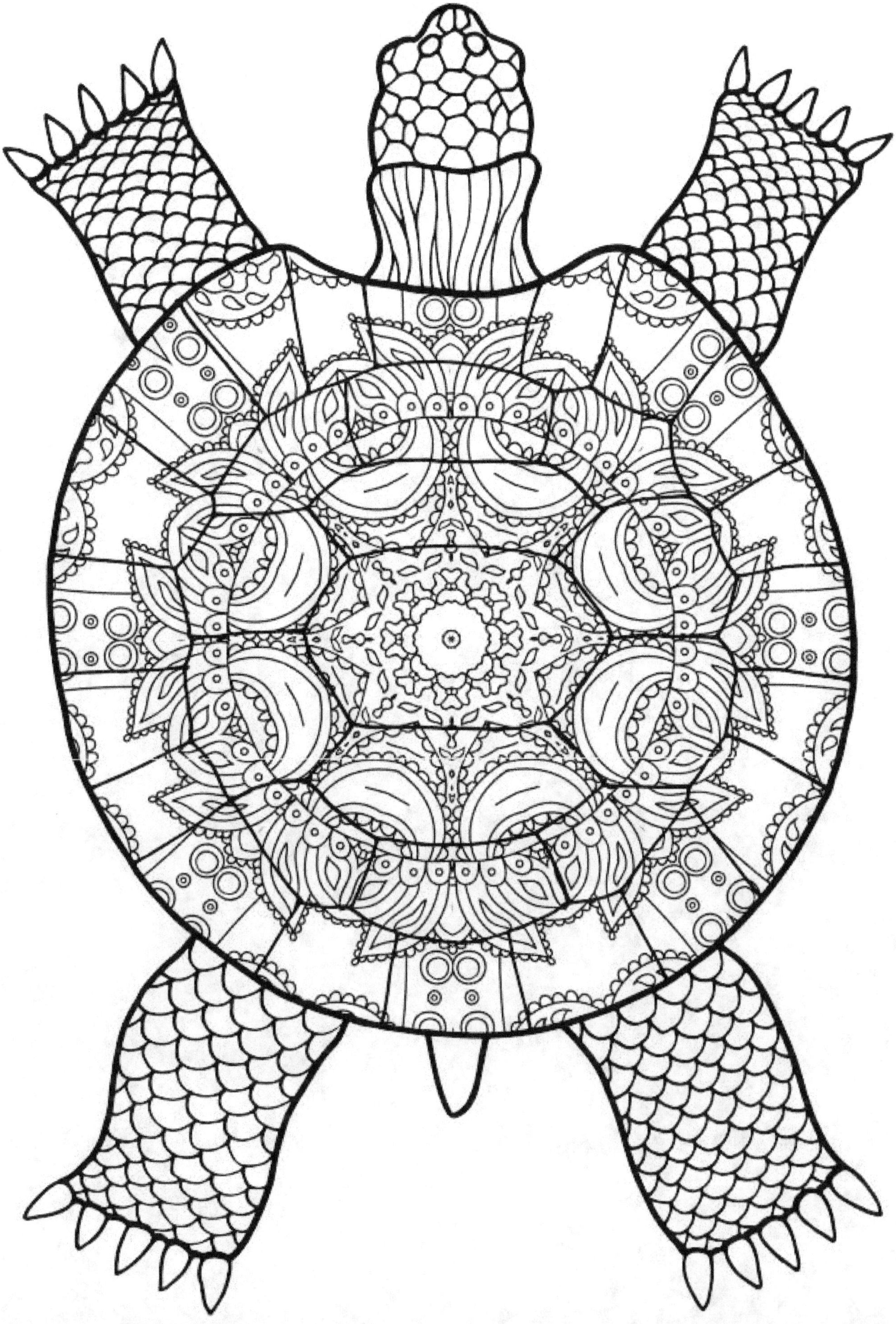

www.ingramcontent.com/pod-product-compliance
Lightning Source LLC
Chambersburg PA
CBHW081213170526
45165CB00009B/2799
9781548158941